THE R

Based on Jon Tuffley's

John Grant, John Robertson, Ricardo Pinto, Rod Grant

GRAPHICS & LAYOUT

Chaz Elliott, James Worrall, Ricardo Pinto

PASTE-UP

Chaz Elliott, James Worrall, Kevin G. McGregor

TYPESETTING

Jared Earle

ARTWORK

James Worrall, Tony Ackland, David Allsop, Andrew Currie, Alan Davidson, Pete Knifton, Colin MacNeil, Kevin G. McGregor, N. Nimmoy, Adrian Smith, Stephen Tappin, Pete Venters, Kevin Walker

COVER

Colin MacNeil

CONCEPTS

James Worrall, Ricardo Pinto, John Robertson, J. Grant, Chaz Elliott

TEXT

Ricardo Pinto

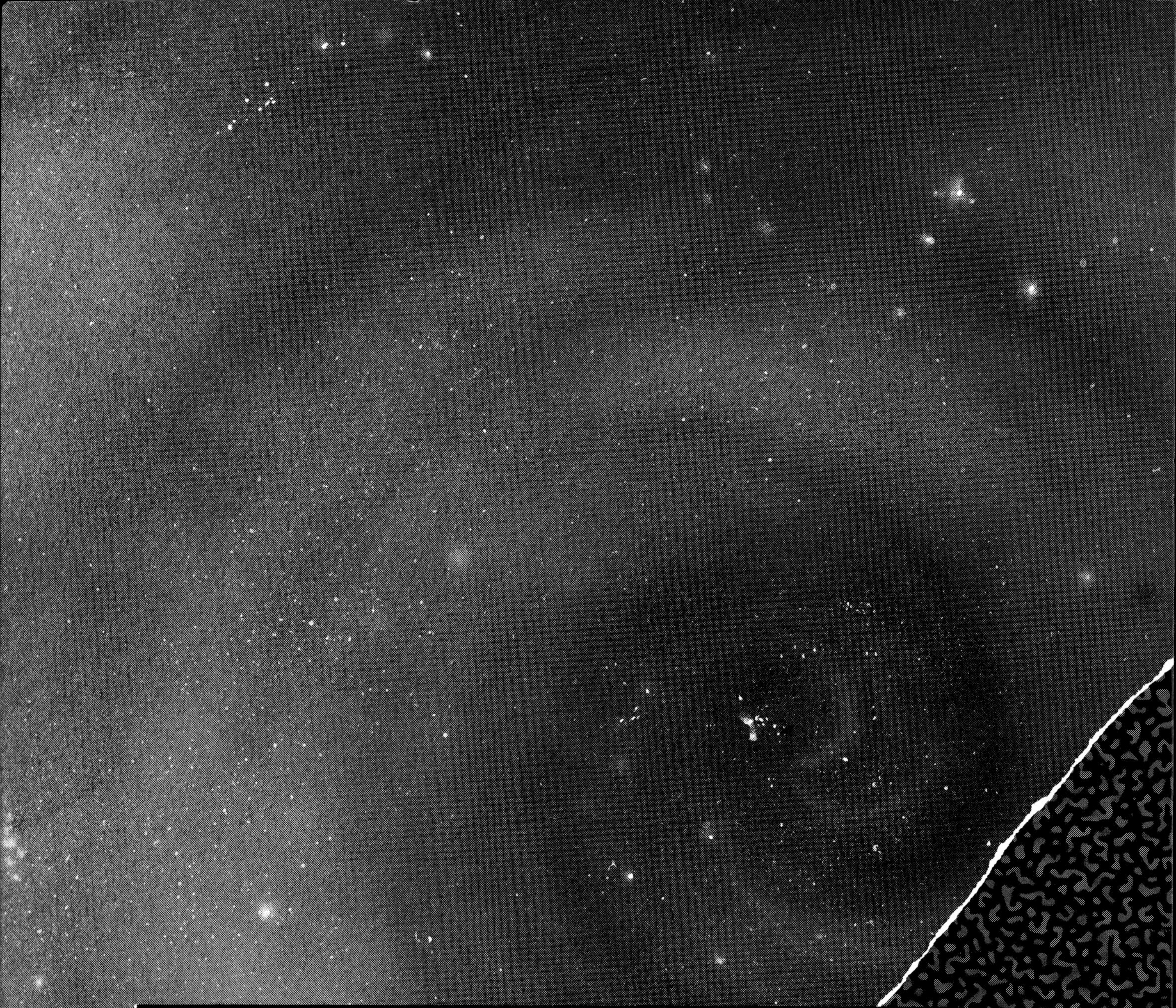

"We live in a dark time. The human species is now engaged in a desperate struggle with a terrible alien enemy. I, like many others throughout the Panhumanic Community, find myself confused and lost in the welter of information and conjecture relating to this matter. This is a collection of articles and papers obtained from a variety of sources that I hope might serve to bring some measure of understanding to those struggling to come to terms with the present crisis."

- Yadis Maruganya: Librarian 2nd Class, Grand Irallic Library, Irallia, 02.08.3493 IST

"It is said that Man is made in the image of God and since this God made the Universe, Humanity feels confident that it has a right to rule it.

But there are other Gods, dark Gods, Gods in whose terrible image other creatures are made -

and these too might believe that they are destined to rule......."

-origin unknown, 34th Century IST

ALIS C031.5

A F 6

3 2 4

9 8 7

CHAPTER 1

The Kryomek - The First Encounter

Entry in the Encyclopaedia Irallica

Encubed Imprint 3490 (Visicube 27.4.tl99)

ALIS D792.43

8	7	0
0	0	0
0	1	1

On 3487 a representative of the megacorp Pandaris Prime informed the Nexus Quorumate that a type 5 shear trajectory had been determined in the Maktor Diman. The first interstice lay in the middle of panhumanic spacetime: the second lay across the galactic centre in a far distant star cluster[1]. The Quorumate financed the sending of a probe through the diman. This returned data by TDC[2] that indicated that the cluster had an unusually high planetation index. The APT[3] provided two of its transmuting vessels and a diman dreadnought was assigned as escort with a full 20 bicentions of troopers and associated support craft. The entire operation was to be commanded by Admiral Mankturian.

The transfer through the manifold was successful and several I-Class planets were quickly located and the planetary transmuting ships were dispatched on ion drive towards the nearest. The process continued in the usual way for several months as the transmutor ships jumped from system to system. Few life-forms were discovered and those that were were exterminated by the repropods[4].

The main fleet was passing through the Jang'ada system and went to examine some signals coming from the vicinity of the gas giant Aleph Jang'ada when the encounter occurred. The third moon of the planet contained an outpost hive of the

---

1 see "Appendix A: Dimensional Manifolds"

2 Trans-Dimensional Carrier used for inter-planetary communications.

3 Agency for Planetary Transmutation (see next footnote)

4 see "The Planetary Transmutation of Avakrellia II"

7

First Encounter

Kryomek. The troopers were completely overwhelmed. Kryomek craft swarmed up from the moon and severely damaged the fleet. Admiral Mankturian only just managed to make it back to the manifold with the dreadnought. Damage to it's space folding equipment caused more losses as the transfer through the diman was partially unsuccessful. At that time the Kryomek did not have any diman technology and they could not follow.

The disaster at Aleph-Jang'ada III re-examined

by Bicenturion Hragnos Baltak

Article Appearing in an Aractosian holomag,

10.01.3491 IST

ALIS C792.43
8 7 0
0 0 0
0 1 1

The day Janduvar 13, 3488 is burned deep in my memory as it is in all the combat troops of the NTFA[5] that took part in the terrible massacre that began on Aleph-Jang'ada III.

I am writing this in an attempt to set the record straight. The subsequent humiliation of Admiral Mankturian at the Court of Investigation that was set up after the battle still rankles with many of his fellow officers. We said it at the time, and I repeat it again now, no man could have avoided the massacre! We were not expecting what happened - and there was no reason to do so. He was just a scapegoat - a sacrifice to the hysteria that flew through the outworlds to eventually reach even the home-worlds.

When the Admiral's task fleet approached the third moon of Aleph-Jang'ada on what was, after all, a routine reconnaissance of a new system it was evident from certain electronic transmissions, that were picked up by the fleet's sensors that there was something on that rock that had at least rudimentary technology. These were run through the decryptor circuits of the compcore[6] time and time again with no result. The messages, if that was what they were, were regular enough for it to appear obvious that they were not a natural phenomena. The compcore could resolve nothing with a linguistic content from the signal patterns.

I must stress that the fleet was immediately put on yellow alert - even though by then it was suspected that this might indeed be some kind of strange natural phenomenon that had never been previously encountered. Cautiously, the Admiral ordered the fleet into a standard conic formation and thus we approached the moon ready for anything .... anything that is except what we found.

At first everything went by the book. The Convict-units were landed by twister[7] before all the others - as usual. I could see the neuro-regulators embedded in their skulls glowing like single, bright eyes - it was because of this that the regular grunts called them 'cyclos'. I could also see the characteristic shapes of their special brand of heavy equipment without all the fancy safety gear that the regulars demanded. They fanned out from their shattered capsules and then we went in behind them - using them as cover - as the manuals instruct us to do. Our power armour was encrusted with the dirt of countless other moons. It was just like any of the others - there was some talk about it all being a joy-ride - some crude jokes - the normal thing - nothing out of the ordinary.

We had been given a fix on the signal as we landed and I was directing several squads of troopers that way when I spotted the chimney. I

5 Nexus Tri-Federational Alliance

6 high yield computer matrix.

7 helical descent landing pod: see "Application of Biostatic Cryogenic Systems to High Velocity Personnel Deployment Systems"

could only see its strangely shaped upper lip over the rim of the crater but as we got closer I saw more of it, and then I saw that it was flanked by others. Then we crested the crater wall and saw it all. There it was as real as you like. The entire crater was full of those strange towers in elaborate clusters, stretching as far as the eye could see - and even further if my sensors were to be believed. It was such a surprise that perhaps we all just stopped - stunned staring at it all - perhaps it was that hesitation that finished us.

For then it happened. There were a hundred flashes amongst the nest of chimneys as a swarm of craft as dense as smoke erupted from amongst the towers. They were upon us before we knew it. It was a nightmare - a nightmare in slow motion without the sound-track. Demons, monstrous terror-creatures fell from the sky, from spined sky-racks, tearing and rending as they fell. Gobbets of thick, scintillating fluid arched through the air and where these landed they burned - even through the rock. Blasts of violet fire punched holes in power armour. Then I saw one of them - one of the things, huge with a head full of teeth. He smashed his way through the cyclos as if they were toys, shredding them like paper dolls. Even to this day I wake up screaming with the image of that horror forever printed on my retina. No need here to describe the Kryomek. Now everyone has heard of them - everyone has seen the hideous *things*. Familiarity has made people blasé to the horror - they're no worse than things on a holopic .. but then few of them have seen them in the flesh - their alien flesh with its lurid, iridescent sheen - their carapaces - the loathsome belch of their weapons - or seen them rending flesh when they feed on human carrion.

I suppose we could be blamed for having become complacent. But then you must remember that we were only escorting a transmuting expedition. We had met other life-forms before.

The Kryomek were the first to fight back.

CHAPTER 2

In the throes of civil strife few eyes were turned up to see the invaders.

Origins of the Nexus Tri-Federational Alliance

Entry in the Encyclopaedia Irallica

Encubed Imprint 3490 (Visicube 13.7.x675)

ALIS C789.1
A 2 5
0 1 1
8 1 8

The Nexus owes its origins to the conditions that existed in the latter half of the 34th century. A certain tension had always existed between the three inhabited worlds orbiting Solarica. Irallia's claim to the mastery of the three relied essentially on it having been the original homeworld of the race. Aractos used its pre-eminent technology to justify its demands for dominance while Xardil, the furthest from the sun and then still a cold and hostile frontier world, boasted that its race were destined for imperial greatness because they were younger and more virile than those who lived on the other two warmer worlds.

For centuries these warlike planets had vied with each other for supremacy and squabbled for control of the double ring of mineral-rich asteroids. Warfare was endemic to the area but it was rare for these conflicts to extend beyond purely stratospheric skirmishes. The inhabitants of all three worlds watched these conflicts in their skies complacently. Fathers pointed out the casualties to their sons as if they were nothing more than a shower of shooting stars.

As the 34th century drew too a close things changed. The population of Irallia always large was expanding explosively. Aractos would take no more immigrants and Xardil had become unattractive even to the poorest Irallian. Colonies had been put on some of the more habitable moons of the gas giants but these would have been expensive even without the constant warfare and became ruinously so with it. Forcible deportation was even tried - though it too failed because of the astronomical cost. Irallia began to

Nexus History

collapse under a flood of humanity. At that time it - like the other two - was a political chaos of democratic pluralism. The people of Irallia were dictated to by the shrill capitalistic demagogues that were really the voices of the exploiting corporate structures that ran the planet. It was a delicate balance, one carefully kept for centuries by rich industrialists. Perhaps they thought that it was going to be like that forever. If so they were wrong. From the most miserable shanty town of the great megatropolis Xirell there rose a messiah. He called himself Qaral which in Saka-Irallic[8] means Purification. To history he is better known as The Flayer.

It took just seventeen days for Qaral to overthrow the system which had controlled Irallia for centuries. His acolytes moved across the planet like a plague whispering rebellion into the ears of the dispossessed. At first the governments thought that they could contain it in Xirell. The city was blockaded and its inhabitants began to starve. But the rebellion was like a pestilence: the weaker the people became the more susceptible they became to the words of the Dark Prophet. Soon he ruled supreme in the ruined megatropolis. His followers, already demented, slipped into madness, painted themselves and even wore the skins of their enemies which they did in mockery of the former exploitations of their oppressors.

The rich began to fear. The mask fell away and all the apparent conflicts between them whether religious or political or whatever else vanished as if they had never been. As it bent all its resources to crushing the Flayer in Xirell the Establishment was revealed unified before the world as it had always been behind the scenes. It was already too late. Rebellion had spread like cancer to the other megatropolises and even into the ranks of the military and security forces. By the seventh day as all semblance of order disappeared, the skins of the rich began to adorn the glass towers from which they had ruled for so long.

The Terror spread. The memories of the multitudes were scoured for records of past crimes and outrage and the acolytes of the Flayer were everywhere casting their unfortunate victims upon the rack.

The rich on the other two planets watched the carnage with ever increasing horror for neither Aractos nor Xardil were strangers to exploitation. They feared that the blight of rebellion might spread across the vacuum to their worlds and they determined that they would step in and cleanse Irallia of it first. The two planets that had been at war for centuries formed an instant alliance and it was only a matter of days before their joint fleets appeared in the skies of Irallia. The planet was defenceless. In the throes of civil strife few eyes were turned up to see the invaders.

Death rained down upon the torn planet. There was no attempt to choose 'military targets'. The Alliance was determined to burn Irallia clean of the dangerous contagion. It began as a punitive attack against the rebels but ended in a holocaust. For days fire fell from the skies until even the great towers of the megatropolises had fallen into the smouldering mass below. The stratecoms of the Alliance considered their strategies and beheld the ruin and sent back reports to their worlds that they were victorious and that the Flayer and his rebellion were no more.

The great fleet returned into the void between the three worlds leaving only a few vessels to police the ruins. On Aractos and Xardil the politicians like the scavengers they were had already begun to carve up Irallia between them.

8 dead classical language used for centuries in divine liturgy.

But the Irallian fleets had not been destroyed. When the Flayer rose from the burning ruins into the sky with his crazed legions the few remaining Alliance ships were easily overwhelmed. Then it was the turn of the Irallians to visit their enemies with fire. The Flayer came amongst them like Death himself, unlooked for and terrifying.

In the end the Alliance managed to repulse the Flayer but at great cost. He returned to Irallia with the battered remnant of his legions. His was a spent force. With his defeat the spell was broken. He vanished from history and Irallia settled into decay. When the Alliance returned the survivors were a few wretches skulking in the ruins leaderless and despairing.

But the Alliance itself had been transformed, forged anew by the terrible price that it too had paid. The old order had been discredited and the victorious military moved into the power vacuum that they left.

The military were led by a group of enlightened men that did not wish to turn Irallia into a slave planet. They found what representatives they could in the ruins of the megatropolises and asked them to bring Irallia into a new Triple alliance. The Nexus Quorumate was formed from the highest ranking stratecoms and admirals of the military of all three planets. These men had the vision to turn their eyes out from the small cluster of three planets to the immensity of the greater galaxy. They understood that Man's destiny lay amongst the stars. Those stars were a prize that seemed ripe for the picking.

The Corporationalising of the Panhumanic Metaconomy

by Anquviar Haldosiac, 21.02.3490 IST

Article appearing in the Muja issue of "The Corporation"	ALIS C793.7 8 4 2 1 0 0 A 0 5
(one of a series of articles dealing with developmental metaconomic issues.)	

The past decade has seen an unprecedented expansion of the panhumanic metaconomy. In this time we have seen an increasing integration between the economic system and the Nexus Military. Of course this is a rather simplistic way of stating what is unsurprisingly a process of great complexity and subtlety. This article will attempt to analyse the basic trends and developments that have led to the current metaconomic system.

Metaconomic transformation began in 3463 when the Nexus Quorumate repealed the anti-monopolistic statutes that formed part of an ancient Irallic Law. This law was originally intended to stop overall control of vital planet wide services from falling into the hands of a few large corporations.

Various adjuncts to this were made when the Triple Alliance was formed that extended its jurisdiction to all three member planets. Simultaneously, the Quorumate annulled an entire complex of statutes and regulations that determined and in many ways constricted all forms of interplanetary trading and economic activity.

The result of these repeals was to engender a new atmosphere of 'laissez-faire' which set in motion the processes that have culminated in the megacorps. Economic agglutination began early with for example the spectacular series of acquisitions and take-overs which led the already large industrial giant Hajunka to develop within two years into the first true megacorp. Others followed until today 73% of the entire panhumanic metaconomy is controlled by just six megacorps.

Natural economic development would not by itself have accounted for the dramatic transformation of the economic scene. The combination of almost complete government non-intervention had to be coupled to the resource dynamics of the Great Push which each year has seen an exponential increase in markets, in the resource and demographic base. The embryonic megacorps found that they could hitch their production volumes to an unlimited theoretical maximum. Even the most resource consuming technology could be developed at astronomic cost because it would be certain to be accommodated within the rapidly growing metaconomy. The megacorps made fantastic profits. Within five years all but three of them had achieved turnovers that exceeded in size the entire panhumanic economy that had existed just a few years before.

It must be pointed out that throughout this period this level of development would not have been possible without the previously unthinkable partnership between the megacorps and the military. The dynamics of the Great Push made the interests of the military identical to those of the megacorps. The symbiosis was perfect and complete. The Quorumate forced psychosocial changes on the whole panhumanic cultural system whose only purpose was to allow the megacorps to achieve an almost total and unhindered policy of exploitation. The megacorps were soon able to manipulate large portions of the panhumanic populations as they already did enormous sectors of the resource base. In return for this consideration the megacorps provided the military with what it needed: steep-gradient development technologies.

For example, in the first year the military were still using tetrospatial vessels with conventional space-folding capabilities but, by the fourth, spin-offs from space-folding communications technologies had made limited access to dimensional manifolds possible; by the eighth year Hajunka had delivered two Leviathan class dreadnoughts to the military that were capable of unlimited access to probability mapped dimensional manifolds. These developments were initially made to reduce the cost of deep space freight transportation but the result was that the military were given the capacity to rapidly redeploy their resources with next to no relativistic phasing being incurred.

The corollary to this is that Pandaris Prime, another of the megacorps, had developed the manifold probing technologies that allowed the essential probability mapping to be carried out for all dimensional manifolds intersecting panhumanic space-time. Of course since dimensional manifolds suffer from probability drift these mappings are transient and the supply of the constant updates to the military provide Pandaris Prime with a substantial portion of its revenues.

In 3470 the 'Six' met on Irallia for discussions about the possibility of mutual cooperation between their megacorps. Out of this meeting there rose ComCorp which was a cartel that was instituted to exclude all other corporations from achieving the status of megacorps. In early 3471 the Six met again and they invited a representative of the Nexus Quorumate to attend. Admiral Ganjivar Tredilion became the first Moderator and thereafter the organisation met regularly.

The presence of the Nexus moderator effectively gave the Quorumate the status of a megacorp. Within two years ComCorp had achieved almost as much political power as the Quorumate itself.

In conclusion, the linking of ComCorp with the Quorumate has provided humanity with strong leadership in every field and is the foundation on which the entire complex of the panhumanic metaconomy rests. If it were not for these power structures it is possible that the panhumanic system might have been completely overturned by the initial attack from the Kryomek. It is unlikely that when Kryomek and Panhumanic space-time intersected defence would have been possible without, for example, the advanced technologies such as dimensional manifold transportation which were a direct result of megacorpic development. The Hivestone Incursion Crisis , a potentially terminal disaster for Humanity, has in fact been successfully incorporated into the Great Push dynamic. The struggle with the Kryomek is now beginning in earnest and its outcome depends on the ruthlessly efficiency of resource exploitation for which the megacorps are largely responsible.

When the Alliance returned the survivors were a few wretches skulking in the ruins, leaderless and despairing.

SOLARICA
HARIBIDIS
ICARUS
ASTARTIS
IRALLIA
ARACTOS
XARDIL
MAHUBA
LEPIS
IXATHOS

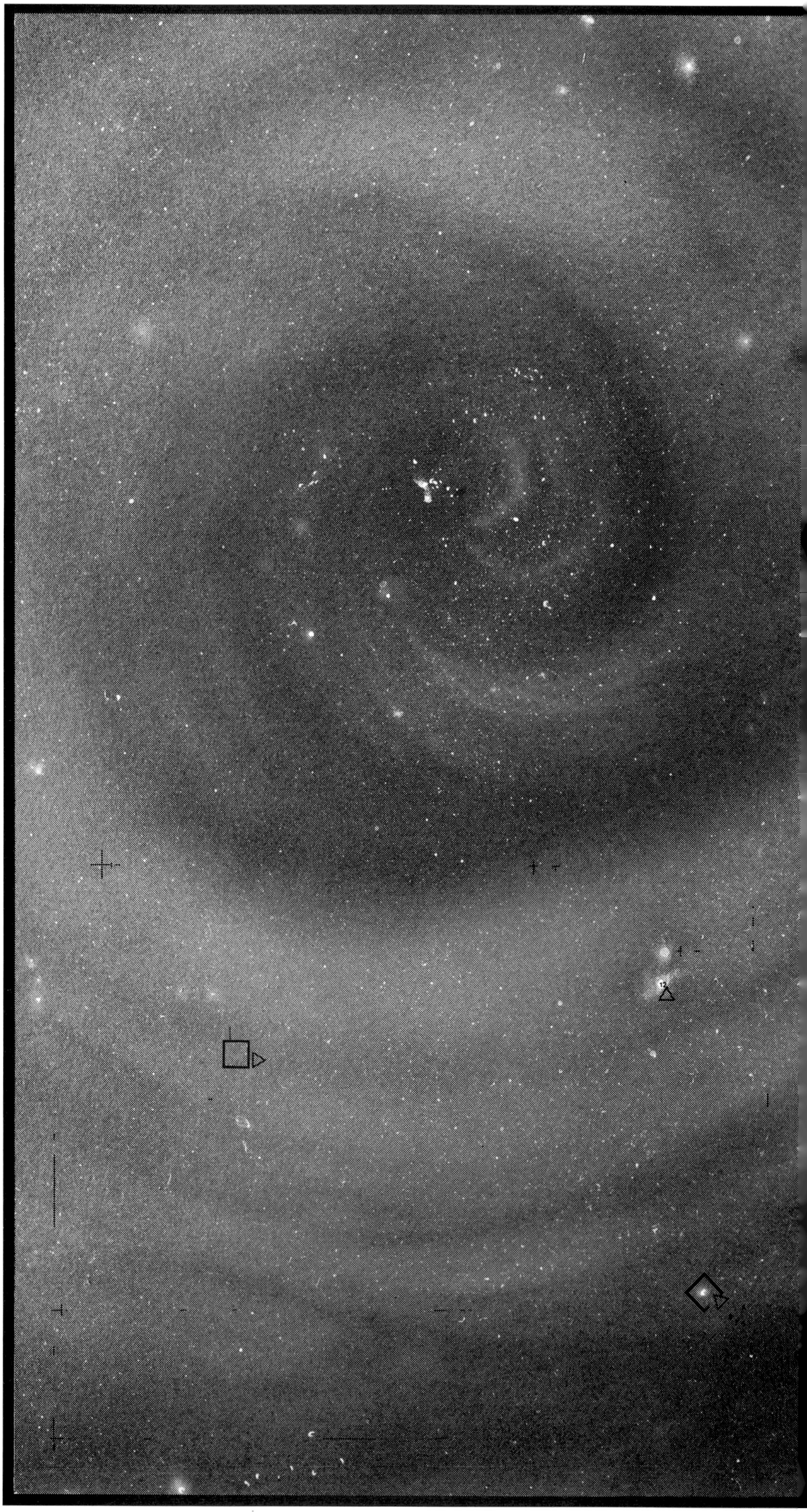
12

ARACTOS

mass (Irallia=1)	0.603
volume (Irallia=1)	0.25
density (water=1)	3.45
Equatorial Diameter (km)	8 998
"Surface" gravity (Ir =1)	0.78
Number of Satellites	3
Period of rotation (Ir days)	1.04
Length of year (Ir days)	23.34
Distance from sun (max) Mkm	202.8
Distance from sun (min) Mkm	181.1
inclination of axis (degrees)	23.41
inclination of orbit to ecliptic	5.4

IRALLIA

mass (Irallia=1)	1
volume (Irallia=1)	1
density (water=1)	5.77
Equatorial Diameter (km)	14 275
"Surface" gravity (Ir =1)	1.00
Number of Satellites	2
Period of rotation (Ir days)	1
Length of year (Ir days)	378.21
Distance from sun (max) Mkm	163.2
Distance from sun (min) Mkm	157.9
inclination of axis (degrees)	21.43
inclination of orbit to ecliptic	0

XARDIL

mass (Irallia=1)	1.204
volume (Irallia=1)	1.11
density (water=1)	5.85
Equatorial Diameter (km)	15 988
"Surface" gravity (Ir =1)	1.12
Number of Satellites	3
Period of rotation (Ir days)	0.92
Length of year (Ir days)	533.23
Distance from sun (max) Mkm	254.3
Distance from sun (min) Mkm	233.2
inclination of axis (degrees)	11.22
inclination of orbit to ecliptic	0.8

A Guide to Solarica

A Short Guide to Panhumanic Space ALIS CD381.2

1 F 6
1 2 1
8 5 A

(extract) imprint 3480

Solarica

Solarica is an apparently quite ordinary yellow dwarf main sequence star. Half of its mass is concentrated in its core creating the pressure and temperature necessary to cause its nuclear reaction.

Icarus and Haribidis

These two tiny worlds are very peculiar in that they form a micro-planetary system by rotating around each other around a common orbital centre. It is likely that they were once a single planet which was split in two by some cometary collision in the distant past. Icarus, the smaller of the two, has an exceptionally large metallic core which comprises 56% of its volume. They are both without atmospheres and suffer from vast extremes of temperatures.

Astartis

Pearl white Astartis is the planet in the Solaric System that most closely resembles Irallia in both volume and mass. However it has a dense atmosphere of carbon dioxide and hydrocarbonic gases which produce an extremely acidic climatology. It has been the dream of many for centuries to transmute this planet - it might soon be attempted.

Irallia

Moons: Nihiri, Jederan

Beautiful turquoise Irallia is the only Solaric planet to have abundant quantities of surface water. In fact 78% of its surface is covered by the vast Tethas Ocean and the Tantaric Inner Sea. Of the four continents Kanda, Ataras, Athurica and Austraka, only the latter does not have a coast on the Inner Sea.

Irallia's vast population is mainly concentrated in the megatropolises around the Inner Sea and the hundreds of oceanic islands that make up the Austrakan archipelago.

Nihiri

The smallest of Irallia's two moons and the largest military base in the Solaric System. It has berthing facilities for three Leviathan class dreadnoughts.

Jederan

The caverns of Jederan contain a dense population. This is the thriving financial centre of Solarica and one of the greatest in all of panhumanic spacetime.

Aractos

Moons: Trakuya, Mendigal, Carbondar

Golden Aractos was originally a cold desert planet with a thin atmosphere. It was here that humanity made its first attempt at planetary transmutation. Centuries have seen Aractos acquiring, through a systematic liberation of all reserves of atmospheric gases, an atmosphere which is now almost indistinguishable from that of its mother planet Irallia. The planetary climate is carefully controlled to minimise cloud cover which thus increases the proportion of Solaric heat reaching the planet surface. In equatorial regions bodies of open water have been created. The vast area of land available for habitation is offset by the great drop in temperature as it gets nearer the poles. On much of Aractos people live very much as they do on Irallia though outside the tropics lifestyles are more reminiscent of Xardil than they are of the mother planet.

The low gravity tends to mean that Aractans are generally a taller, slenderer race. Certain conditions attendant on the original colonies have left Aractos at the forefront of human technologies.

Trakuya

Owned by the Agarax corporation highly cyberneticized and protected by one of the most sophisticated security systems in panhumanic space. Cerabex is located here: this is the birthplace of the famous active cyberneural matrix.

The Moloch Rings

The two rings of asteroids, Moloch Minor and Moloch Major support a large thriving population of miners. The Rings are very mineral rich and it is true to say that the panhumanic colonisation would not have been possible without them. The population of the Molochs is not distributed uniformly throughout the rings but rather is concentrated on the larger asteroids. Of these the two most notable are Darkstone and Kutta which are renowned for their violence and debauchery.

Xardil

Moons: Gulgatrax, Makoydis, Uris, Lucifer,

Xardil is likely to remain an anomaly amongst human colonised worlds because it is no longer necessary to colonise worlds so inhospitable to human beings. From space Xardil appears to be a rusty red - this is a peculiarity of its rocks and soils that contain a substantial proportion of ferrous compounds. This world is very cold and unlike its sister planet Aractos, no attempt was made to transmute it. In spite of this Xardil is densely populated though the majority of the population is found beneath the planet surface. There are thousands of population centres connected by surface maglevs and the people show a resilience which has made Xardillians bear a disproportionate burden of the colonisation of the Outworlds. The heavier gravity has made the standard Xardillian noticeably squatter and more muscular than his Irallic brother.

Gulgatrax

The high security prison moon where the most dangerous criminals from a thousand worlds are incarcerated.

Lucifer

The headquarters of the megacorp Hajunka and it is here that the first Leviathan class dreadnoughts were built in orbit.

Mahuba

Moons: Tatun, Kakar, Gigaltion, Sulphuria, Yantiri, Alkolan, Mesmurian, Pantegron, Yadris, Momandron, Polgonoth, Tognoth, Artica, Bazedus, Zeduphar, Pagaja, Kintikor, Feyada,

Since ancient times this red gas giant has been associated with the dark procreation gods of many cultures. When the first telescope trained on its blood red eye it was to find the most violent storm centre in the Solaric System.

Polgonoth

A huge astrophysics and astronomic research establishment is situated here listening and watching the cosmos.

Lepis

Moons: Hrilli, Takeda, Dangoran, Neptunia, Okania, Marussia, Tritonus, Ammonuria, Methana, Jangis-Tur, Haheda, Iapatus

Sea green Lepis is a mysterious world that has only ever been visited by probes. It seems to have a core of liquid hydrogen and exhibits bizarre large scale perturbations in its magnetic field.

Ixathos

Moon: Hadis

Tiny Ixathos is so far from Solarica that for much of its year its atmosphere which is mainly composed of methane becomes frozen. It exhibits the peculiar phenomena called the 'lights' which is caused by electrical discharges through the substantial quantities of atmospheric neon. The eccentricity of its orbit sometimes brings it within the orbit of Lepis.

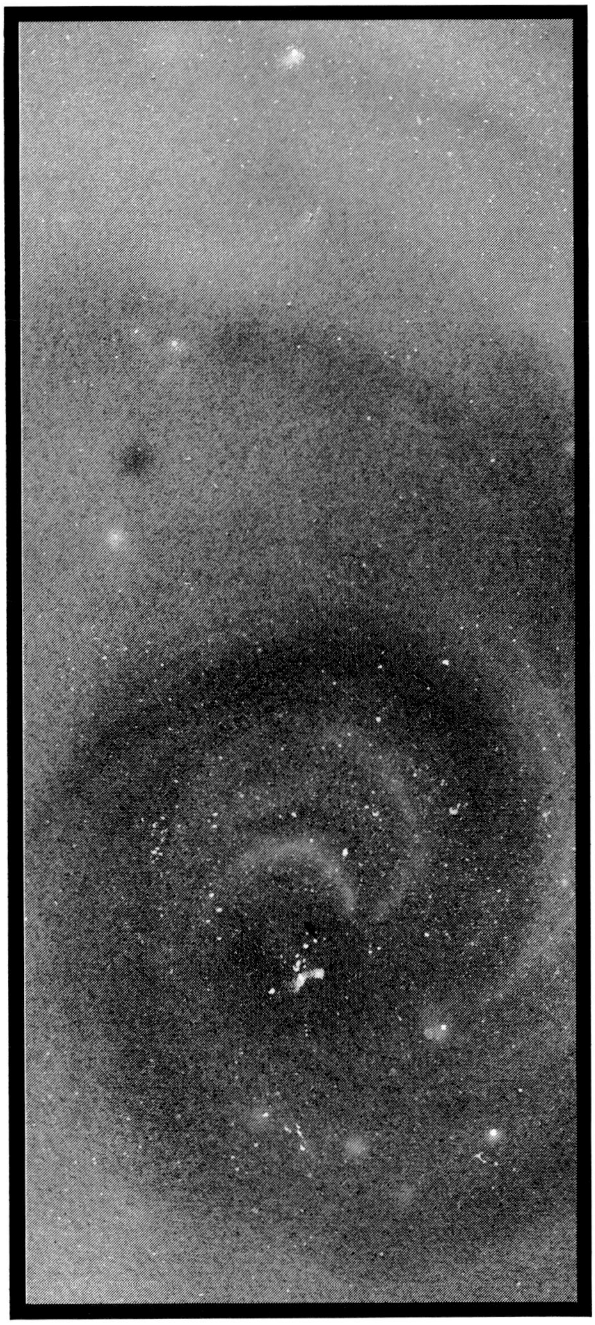

CHAPTER 3

Kryomek Biogenetics

Entry in the Encyclopaedia Irallica

Encubed Imprint 3490 (Visicube 12.3.ff8)

ALIS CA587.3
0 0 7
0 0 1
1 F 6

Biogenetical knowledge concerning the Kryomek is still at a fairly rudimentary stage. All information currently available is derived from the analysis of the data obtained during the recent Hivestone Incursion Crisis[9]. No specimen has ever been taken alive and very few were obtained intact from the battlefield. In addition the examination of a dead Kryomek is fraught with difficulties - not least the highly corrosive nature of its body fluids. Putrefaction sets in remarkably quickly and all of the really valuable data was obtained actually on the battlefield before the carcass had time to decompose too far.

However certain things are known. For example it has been ascertained beyond any doubt that the Kryomek consist of a variety of sub-species which are all trimorphic (that is they all pass through three distinct stages of body development). That they have three 'sexes' is now considered beyond doubt. Most Kryomek are predominantly of the neuter sex class. Each hive is dominated by a Hivemaster, an enormous winged creature that performs the function which in our terms might be labeled, 'male'. Biologically speaking, its function is predominantly one of impregnating the vast, bloated breeders. These in turn function as enormous egg factories that produce the endless

The Kryomek

WARRIOR

WARMASTER

numbers of Kryomek of the neuter sex class. Beyond the Hive much power is devolved to other huge winged creatures called Swarmmasters. Swarmmasters are almost indistinguishable from a Hivemaster but they do not appear to perform any sexual function and remain subservient to them. They have the ability to be able to produce all the essential chemical signals that control the Hive Swarm.

The three distinct forms found in the Kryomek warrior caste occur in a regular succession. The Helion form originates from its egg as a primitive eating machine. Its very lack of higher functions makes it an awesome assault weapon. It seems to be by feeding on the flesh of the Hive's victims that the bio-genetic changes are induced in the Helion that cause it to pass through a pupation stage to become a Warrior.

The Warrior is a fearsome creature of marked intelligence and weapon handling ability. It is not known what precipitates some Warriors to transform into the third and final stage, the Warmaster. These are monstrous horrors - terrifyingly aggressive, cunningly intelligent and very powerful, having lost their legs and developed an armoured carapace and tail.

Close analysis of visidata obtained from the remains of the partially completed Hive on Tau-Maktor suggests that the Kryomek had begun to construct hybrid composites by geno-splicing together the scavenged parts of Kryomek and Human troops.

Though very little direct evidence exists it is assumed that the Helion form must also be capable of transforming into the numerous Hivebrood, or worker caste, that perform non-combative functions in the Hive.

Organisation and Structure in a Kryomek Hive (Extract)

Report presented to the Nexus Military Quorumate by the NMI

ALIS BA587.2
1 2 A
0 0 1
2 5 A

NMI_SR22245/Dept 5.3/05.05.3492

All Kryomek biological functions, biopolitical structures and military organisation are based around the complex infrastructure which, for lack of a better term, is called a hive. The common analogy used to describe these hives is to compare them to human cities - this analogy is fallacious - in fact these vast structures bear little resemblance to anything previously encountered by the Nexus Tri-Federation.

It must be said at the outset that all the data that has been collected on this subject is very meagre and, considering the threat that the Kryomek pose to humanity, it is pitifully inadequate.

Some information was obtained by those few of our operatives that we have actually managed to get into a Hive. This policy has been discontinued because of the unsustainable losses in manpower (see attached Addendum 6 [10]). The other main source of information comes from members of the

9 see "The Hivestone Incursion Crisis"

10 this addendum has been excluded from the present work in the interests of brevity.

MACNEIL '91

NTFA forces that have penetrated Hives during military encounters - **and survived**.

Architecturally all hives so far encountered seem to be remarkably similar and probably conform to patterns that are genetically encoded into the Hivemaster that oversees its construction. Ostensibly, most of the hive lies below the surface - at this time we have no way of ascertaining how deep they go. On the surface there are densely packed clusters of hexagonal tubes - some form towering 'chimney's' that presumably are used to expel wastes from the hives and perhaps to draw in various atmospheric gases. Others are the ends of huge shafts that plunge deep into the earth. From these the Swarms of Kryomek craft issue out from the hive.

Beneath the surface all that we know suggests that the hive consists of vast interlocking flat discs each consisting of innumerable chambers and centred on one of the vertical shafts. There are various conjectures as to how the discs are interconnected. It is also thought likely that there are deep sub-structures of the hive that are connected to shafts that do not reach the surface.

The hivecore is the complex of chambers that houses the Hivemaster and his entourage. It is probably always located quite deeply in the hive and will have direct connections with the numerous brood chambers which contain the breeders and the millions of eggs.

Only one hivecore has ever been penetrated by NTFA personnel - a specially trained suicide convict-squad[11]. (There is no reason at this time to suppose that this was not a typical example.) The hivecore was very deep - at least 2.5 kilometres below the surface - and seemed to be of vast extent. Careful scrutiny of the visicube data obtained by the squad before they stopped transmitting has revealed how intricate and deeply organised the structure is. The Hivemaster has now been located and identified on the visidata and when this was obtained, it was being evacuated by a detachment of huge Warmasters.

Careful structural analysis of the data has revealed a structure which we have termed the Hub. This was at the centre of a bewildering array of instruments of bio-mechanical construction - beyond this in concentric rings of ever increasing diameter were numerous instruments and fantastically mutated Kryomek hivebrood and other organisms that were imperceptibly fused with the machinery surrounding them. Our scientists are convinced that this elaborate nerve centre responds to the Hivemaster at its centre in much the same way that a body does to its brain.

11 the Hivestone during the Hivestone Incursion Crisis

The Hivemaster lies in the hub exuding control substances which are picked up by batteries of chemical amplifiers and which transmit his commands throughout the hive. Other sensors and instruments allow commands to be issued to distant Swarmmasters. From a hub of this kind an Imperial Hivemaster could have bi-directional chemical linkages with all his Swarmmasters in the field, with Swarmfleets and with vassal Hivemasters. It is highly probable that contact is even maintained with the other five Imperial Hivemasters that apparently make up the directing will of the Great Hive Hegemony.

One of the brood chambers was briefly penetrated providing us with the only visidata available. The breeder was a vast bloated bag crawling with small Kryomek hivebrood. Innumerable chambers led from it each filled with eggs of different sizes - many were connected to equipment which suggests that they are artificially incubated.

There are two other salient features that should be noted. The first is that NTFA squads have encountered areas which seem to function as some kind of hibernation chamber with vast banks of cells each occupied by a Kryomek of the warrior caste. Brief examination revealed evidence that these Kryomek were in some kind of state of suspended animation - perhaps to be activated by a control substance produced by their Hivemaster.

The second feature of particular interest, and a source of some distaste was the discovery of chambers whose function seems to be connected with the construction of Kryomek hybrids... hybrids that appear to incorporate the scavenged component parts of both Kryomek and ... **of human troops.**

The Origins of the Advanced Kryomek Hive Complex

by Jardus Manturikan

Article Appearing in Scientific Xardillian ALIS B587.19
B 3 9
0 1 1
Actabros 3492 IST 3 7 A

It is impossible at this time to ascertain even a vague date as to when it was that the present Great Hive system arose amongst the various subspecies of the Kryomek though, without doubt, this period must lie well in antiquity. Furthermore it is purely a matter of conjecture as to exactly what planet gave birth to this virile life form. Statistical correlation of all known Kryomek occupied worlds has lead to a number of projections which would place the homeworld somewhere in the Bayuda-Manturax Karyx 5 subquadrant. Certainly the homeworld of the Kryomek species must have had a high predation index, perhaps well into the 40s, to account for the extreme adaptations possessed by the Kryomek for conquest and other-species annihilation.

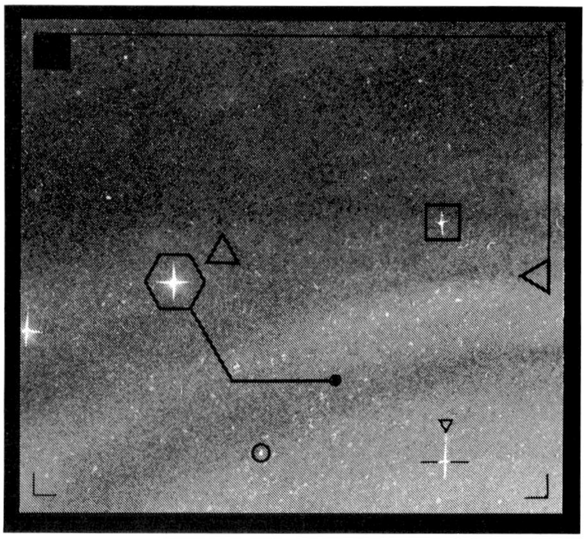

The current Great Hive meta-structures show a high degree of sophisticated scientific advancement which, however, appears to be completely integrated with many ancient features of a fundamentally bio-genetic nature.

The Proto-Hive systems were essentially bio-genetic ones with the maintenance of a vast and continuous spawning rate being the central dominating force driving all further development. It is certain also that this constant population pressure led to an ever increasing conflict for resources which led in turn to unremitting internecine warfare which finally culminated in the bio-militaristic mechanisms which are the present Great Hives.

At all times in their history it must be assumed that the Kryomek were entirely dominated by their Hivemasters. Because of the bio-genetic centrality of the Hivemasters, all subsequent developments necessarily led automatically into an increase in their power and sophistication.

For example, before the Kryomek developed chemical synthesizer-transducer technologies, the size of a hive was limited by the amount of control substances that could be produced by the Hivemaster and the maximum range over which these could be dispersed. The development of sophisticated dispersal techniques, by itself might have led the way for an immediate and massive expansion of hive systems. Coupled with chemical amplifying technologies the development of enormous hive systems seems inevitable.

The most important consequence however of these developments was the emergence of the Great Hive System. The new chemicoms systems not only allowed a vast increase in the size of a hive but also the distance at which a Hivemaster could maintain intimate chemical communication and control of his Swarmmasters.

One other core advance, essential to the emergence of the Great Hive System, was the gradual evolution of Imperial Hivemasters. It is certain that from the beginning Hivemasters had, at certain times caused to be produced other Hivemasters to take their closely allied genetic strain and form a new hive. This new hive though having strong bio-genetic links with the parent Hive, would certainly have become rapidly independent. The new technologies however allowed a Hivemaster to exploit a certain advantage that was always inherent in the spawning of new Hivemasters. A Hivemaster that nurtured the spawning of another creature like itself would soon have found itself the target of its offsprings voracious appetites if it were not that evolution had provided a 'chemical backdoor', a substance produced by a Hivemaster that maintained control over the new Hivemasters even as they emerged from their eggs. This control would last until they left the hive. Once the substance was no longer present the new Hivemaster rapidly threw off its vassalage to its parent.

The new chemicom systems however, allowed the parent Hivemaster to maintain its offspring in perpetual thraldom by transmitting the control substance to them constantly - these Imperial Hivemasters came to dominate an ever increasing brood of junior Hivemasters and so could form a super hive system - or what is technically termed a Great Hive.

visicube 6-MR/3 - [22:14:05] 19/07/3489 IST
operation code: M256.45 DD07/XM4-C01-S19
location: Kryomek Hivestone - Maktor 000
subject: [Hivemaster] - hub - hivecore

Pete Venters 91

Bio-Political Power Structures of the Great Hive Hegemony (An extract)

Doctoral Thesis 3493 - Ambuvar Mercatos Brandillian -(Extract)	ALIS B587.2 4 4 D 1 2 4 2 9 E
Chandar University, Aractos	

Any analysis of the structure of the Great Hive Hegemony has to contend with the sparsity of data available on all matters concerning the Kryomek. However, even though this is the case there are several strong reasons why I have chosen to examine this topic. Not least amongst these is the fact that humanity has never before been in a position to properly examine a virile alien culture - especially one of such complexity.

There is one singular component of Kryomek politics that is unique - and that is the bio-genetic paradigm that is at its centre. The most paradoxical and fascinating manifestation of this is the Great Hive Hegemony itself.

Clearly it would be presumptuous of me to suggest that I have a deep understanding of how the Hegemony works but rather I would like to suggest some possible explanations for the observed facts.

Firstly, the Hegemony is composed of the six creatures which are normally termed the Imperial Hivemasters. Each of these is the lord of a Great Hive, an absolute monarch whose each and every chemical exudation is received with fanatical fervour by his subjects as a command from a god. The peculiarity in this, at least from the position of a comparative political analyst, is that all the subjects of an Imperial Hivemaster are also his progeny - even though they are often numbered in their countless billions. Thus an Imperial Hivemaster appears before the other Five as the father and champion of his (and his subjects) paramount genetic lineage.

Power relationships within a Great Hive have been examined in some depth by other researchers, but power relationships within the Hegemony are still shrouded in mystery. It is true that the Six do in some way formulate a common policy for the species. It appears that now there is little internecine conflict between the Great Hives. It seems certain however that this was not the case in the past. Junior Hivemasters are apportioned rights of conquest of new planets by their Overlord - but he in turn must ultimately, in some way, receive this mandate from the Hegemony.

It is possible that the Six carry out a subtle dialogue with chemical messages, remotely from the dark depths of their hives - that when they act, they act in concert - as council, or a debating forum.

And yet, I think not - I cannot support this hypothesis. I would suggest that everything that we know about the Kryomek flies in the face of this supposition. Where is there any evidence that the Kryomek ever indulge in debate? For the Kryomek all is monologue, a perpetual stream of chemically coded imperatives that has been delivered from the cores of their hives since they evolved on some world, distant in both time and space. Everything beats to the insistent rhythm of biological necessity. Their religion is evolution. They live to breed and conquer. In this scheme there is no place for debate, no time for individuality only the single purpose of perpetuating their genetic strain.

I propose to solve this riddle by suggesting that the Six in some way which may possibly always to be beyond the scope of our investigations, in some dark way they choose one from amongst themselves and elect him Hegemon - and then the others for the moment, until the streams of power run in different courses - the others will allow themselves to have his control substances applied to themselves and obey him as their vassals obey them.

I postulate that in all their evolutionary history this ability of an Imperial Hivemaster to temporarily overcome the almost irresistible compulsions to completely and absolutely dominate all other creatures - to make itself subservient to the dictates of another, competing genetic lineage - this would stand out as the greatest landmark for that species. This alone would demonstrate a terrifying clarity of purpose, such a distillation of malice - of an overweening single-minded pursuit of power which would bode ill for all other creatures in this galaxy.

The question I am forced to ask is whether we humans would sink our lesser differences so easily?

The Kryomek War Machine

(transcribed extract from recording of introductory lecture given by Planetary Stratecom Tarandon to officers of the NTFA)	ALIS CB587.4 1 3 3 0 1 4 0 B 6

10.01.3491 IST

An approach which tried to explain the Kryomek by using analogies based on Humanity is one that is bound to fail. The approach of all researchers has been the same. They begin by dividing the Kryomek into categories based on roles and functions. They then proceed to determine the dynamics between those roles and then through this they attempt to arrive at an analysis of the political division of power. Such an approach has little application to the Kryomek. It is never more misguided than when we consider the Kryomek approach to war.

To talk about a Kryomek 'military', to draw a comparison with the NTFA is to commit the greatest of errors. There is no such thing. The nature of the Kryomek is that nothing is divisible. The Kryomek have no military in the same way that they have no government nor economy.

We will begin to reach some measure of understanding if we conceive of the Kryomek as consisting of a few super-organisms. All the Kryomek of one Hive form a single, indivisible organism that has as its 'brain' the Hivemaster and of which the numerous hivebrood and warrior castes form the organs and limbs. Taking this analogy further we can see that the chemical transducer systems that relay control substances play the part of the nervous system. If we take this analogy still further we realise that the Hivemaster does perform all the functions of a brain....exactly! Everything from conscious motivation to exuding the chemicals that like hormones affect the 'rate of growth' and the 'metabolic rate' of the hive.

We can enlarge our model to describe a Great Hive as a super-organism. It is a larger, more powerful form of the hive organism - one that is its evolutionary descendant. Perhaps a comparison might be made here to human mitochondria[12] that are now organs in each and every human cell and which were once independent algal organisms.

Armed with this new powerful analogy we can begin to examine the nature of the Kryomek 'war machine'. It is immediately obvious that when we consider 'warfare' we are not dealing with a special function of the Great Hive super-organism. Warfare is as endemic to it as the action of our immune systems is to us. The Kryomek do not 'declare war' - in fact it is true to say that the Kryomek have no conception of peace - for them all is perpetual struggle. A description of the Kryomek War Machine is in fact a description of the Kryomek themselves!

How then do we describe the motivations of the Kryomek super-organism? The language of Bio-evolution provides us with some help. It is an en-

---

12 organelles in animal cells responsible for metabolic processes.

tity that strives to survive at all costs and to spread its particular genetic strains across as much of spacetime as is possible.

The important thing that we must bear in mind is that a hive is composed of creatures that are genetically kaleidoscopic fragments of their Hivemaster. Only the Hivemaster and breeders are important as the source of the Hive genes - all other members of the Hive are expendable - their only value lying in the investment of time and resources that their body represents.

Incidentally, as an aside, during the Hivestone Incursion we found this to our cost when we attempted to destroy the hive on Tau-Maktor by using nucleonic impact devices launched directly from orbit. At first we were overjoyed when we perceived that all the chimneys and tower stacks were obliterated. I volunteered to go down with the cyclo myriad. We went in by twister. It was cumbersome negotiating the debris of the tower stacks in isolation suits. The ground had been vitrified into a polished mirror by the nucleonic blast. It was like walking on ice. When we approached the ragged lip of the first shaft we could see that the blast must have penetrated deep into the hive. As far as we could see down into the shaft everything had the same reflective, glassy shell - as if someone had spilt a pot of varnish over the whole damn place.

But then they came at us. It was true that the Warmaster's carapaces had lost their gleam. They were scorched and blistered. Their markings were dulled. But they could still fight. They might be slowed by blast trauma but we were encumbered with our isolation suits. I was lucky to get out with my life.

Sure, they would all die in a few weeks - perhaps even days. No living thing - not even a Kryomek can take that kind of dose of gamma rays and remain in the peak of health. But in the end it made no difference. We only stopped them when we incinerated their Hivemaster in the Hivestone itself.

But I digress. As I was saying, the Hivemaster and the Breeders are really the only thing that matter. You can kill everything else but as long as those remain they will rebuild the hive within weeks.

To return to our analogy - it is obvious that blasting off a limb of a super-organism that can regenerate can only give us a local, temporary advantage. Only taking out the brain kills the super-organism - or if that is impossible then go for the nerve centres - for at least these will slow the regeneration. All this is true for the Kryomek whether we are considering assault on a hive, attacking a Swarmfleet or the battlefield Swarm.

On the battlefield the Kryomek have achieved what human military theorists have been attempting for centuries - perfect control. Our forces are subdivided into squads, centions and myriads. All of this is an attempt to suppress the individuality of each soldier and bend his will to the tactical dictates of a single mind. The Kryomek have no need to make such distinctions. They are biogenetically designed to function as a single entity. It is true that they do have something approximating a command structure. In the field the Swarm is controlled by a Swarmmaster, but he relays his instructions to the Warmasters. This appears to have similarities to our military practise. There is no real similarity though, for each Warmaster acts merely as an extension of his

Swarmmaster. There is no notion of jurisdiction except in so far as the dispersal range of the warmaster's control substances determines the effective range of his control. The Swarmmaster passes his helions and warriors from one Warmaster to another as easily as I can move my arm thus....

Kryomek Somatogenic[13] Weapon Systems

by Jardus Manturikan

Article Appearing in Scientific Xardillian ALIS AD587.386
8 2 7
0 0 1
(Extract) Indavas 3493 IST 0 F B

Recent research has revealed the startling fact that many Kryomek battlefield weapons are somatogenic. Many early observers, when confronted with Kryomek bioacid sprays could not understand where the weapon's fluids were stored. Various propositions were put forward suggesting that the Kryomek had developed some kind of molecular compression technology - though no theoretical work could even begin to determine how this was done. The truth is simpler and yet even more astounding than that. The reservoirs for the bioacids were always in view - the bodies of the Kryomek themselves.

Much Kryomek weaponry is metabolically integrated into the creature's soma[14]. Nexus troops had long known that Kryomek blood or - more accurately - serum was highly corrosive but the connection was not made with the weapon propelled bioacids for those were far more powerful. The discovery that such a weapon contained what turned out to be an acid amplifier immediately suggested the Kryomek serum as the most likely source of the bioacids. This theory had the further advantage that it explained why Warmasters were the only Kryomek ever observed to wield the terrifying corroder lance - simply because they had far larger somatic reserves of serum.

More recently it has even been suggested that some of the more complex weapons such as the plasmid cloud-duster are also somatogenic. It is conjectured that the highly infective plasmid vectors are obtained either from a Warmaster's serum or even from a special metabolically integrated implant. In either case the plasmids must be deliberately introduced since they are obviously biogenetically engineered.

13 generated within the body 14 body

The reservoirs for the bioacids were always in view... the bodies of the Kryomek themselves.

CHAPTER 4

Like great fish they swam around the planet and gorged on the assembled resources of humanity.

The Colony Arks

Panhumania (extract)

Educational Imprint 3464 IST

ALIS D781
A F 1
1 1 1
3 1 8

The New Millenium Manifesto was announced on all three homeworlds simultaneously shortly after the formation of the Nexus Military Quorumate. The body of the Manifesto was somewhat complex and tedious but it was preceded by a short passage which is now termed the Panhumanic Declaration. The first few words of this declaration still resound with a resonance which is undimmed by the years.

"As the representatives of the new paramount order we assert that Man's destiny lies in the stars. We say this now that future men shall know where this great thing began and why. We shall begin the struggle now that will give to our children and to our children's children the great immensity of space. They shall be heirs to this great endeavour. Their birthright shall not be denied them."

The Quorumate set about fulfilling their great project immediately. All resources not needed for the reconstruction of Irallia were channelled into the building of the Colony Arks. Nine thousand citizens, three thousand from each of the home-worlds were chosen to carry humanity to the New World. The greatest minds were drawn together to counsel the designers. The skeletons of the three great Arks began to appear in the skies of Aractos. Like great fish they swam around the planet and gorged on the assembled resources of humanity. Three years were spent and the wealth of the race expended. The launching of this first great colonising effort by humanity was timed to coincide with the celebrations that would accompany the ending of the millenium. The Arks were to be a great symbol of hope for the new millenium.

The Great Push

The great day came at last. The Nine Thousand were feted and blessed and then stepped aboard the Arks. All eyes on Aractos turned upwards. The pulse engines, each larger than the fallen towers of Irallia, fired and spat ions into the void. Slowly at first the great mass of the Arks was coaxed into motion. They drifted slowly out of orbit with Aractos. Within twelve days they were sailing past Xardil - already their speed was greater than any that man had attained. Soon they had become three distant shining specs like stars as they passed the great gas giants. Several weeks later they passed through the orbit of tiny icy Ixathos and were officially in deep space.

The colonist Arks sailed through space towards the star Tetaris more than a parsec away. Instruments pointed there had detected a I-class planet. This was to be the New World Tetaris IV.

Avoiding a Demographically Induced Cusp Catastrophe

Report presented to the Nexus Military Quorumate by the TCDS

ALIS A617.3
7 7 A
F 1 0
E 1 7

TCDS_SR4333/DS-21-x/w-33/31.1.3461

The current population increase trends on the three homeworlds of Aractos, Xardil and Irallia threaten to overwhelm the political and economic superstructures of the Nexus Tri-Federational Alliance. An extensive program of investigation has made it fairly certain that the current demographic profile for the three worlds is approaching a saddlepoint cusp which will precipitate the Nexus Tri-Federation into a catastrophe where there will be fast and irrevocable decline in economic and military strength, accompanied by a complete dissolution of social order. Calculations suggest that if the incidence angle of the demographic profile is modified carefully the catastrophe might be avoided and in fact might be led into a rising segment of the saddlepoint cusp.

This solution which is currently termed the Slide-Cusp Scenario involves a number of rapid changes in the way in which otherworld colonisation is being carried out. At the moment this is a haphazard affair with various Tri-Fed. departments and numerous of the larger corporations being involved in an anarchic free for all.

This must change - it must be replaced by a highly coordinated, centralised program of colonisation (our department for Propaganda has suggested calling it the 'Great Push'). Large segments of the homeworld populations must be transplanted to ever further outworlds according

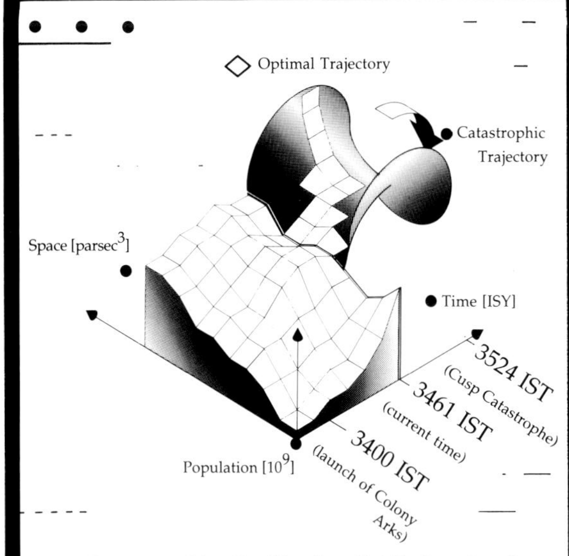

Demographic Profile for Tri-Federational Alliance plotted against space (in cubic parsecs) and through time. The diagram shows the computed demographic surface and the inherent saddlepoint cusp. The probable demographic trajectory is shown as a tesselated path.

to a mathematically precise hyper-trajectory. If this rate of colonisation is not reached then the critical angle of incidence for the demographic profile will not be reached and the plunge into catastrophe will be inevitable.

At this juncture we have to point out that this hyper-trajectory has been plotted and that it demands a colonisation rate of 120 ps/y[15]. As you will immediately realise, this figure is at least 7 times greater than previous ones. In fact it is so high that it seems at first sight to be impossible.

An intense study was immediately initiated to define the limiting parameters of the Great Push - if such existed. This study has now produced its first results. The precise mathematical description is attached separately as it requires a holocube for demonstration. Here we shall just present the main results.

1. The space-time geometry of the Great Push must approximate to a hyper-spherical attractor as much as possible - with the spatial diameter increasing smoothly with the temporal.

2. The outer spherical shell of the Great Push, which will precede the colonists must be 'cleansed'. By this we mean that it must be made ready for the colonists arrival - this will mean that the forces of the NTFA must totally eliminate all other intelligent life on these planets - if any such exists - the geometry of the Great Push cannot handle the singularities that would be produced by inter-species conflict.

This will clearly entail a large increase in the power and strength of the military. It will almost certainly be necessary to form extra auxiliary units from criminals and other malcontents to be used as shock troops - the cost to the military might otherwise become unsupportable.

3. The power of the military must be balanced and partially countered by a similar increase in the powers of all the business interests represented by the large corporations. This will hopefully be achieved by relaxing any Tri-Fed legislation that in any way interrupts the exploitation by the business community of whatever or whomever they desire. (Our preliminary historio-economic calculations indicate that these will necessarily occur within the confines of the Military hyper-boundary - and also that a symbiotic relation will eventually arise between the two. Further data on this will soon be forwarded for your consideration).

4. All peoples of the homeworlds must be whipped into a frenzy of colonial fervour. This must be achieved by a complete control of all channels of communication. A new all-embracing Propaganda Agency must be set up with the dual purposes of conditioning the populations to prevent colonialism and, most importantly, to keep all knowledge of any otherspecies' annihilations that are being carried out by the military completely secret. The colonists must, at all costs, think that the worlds they are setting out for have not and never have had indigenous, intelligent life. This will foster a bright feeling of optimism and opportunity which will act as an important component of the Great Push. A spirit of mistrust for otherworld life-forms must be fostered which will make the colonists treat all alien life as vermin - uniform confidence in all things human is essential.

15 planetary systems per year.

Interstellar Colonisation - The early years

	ALIS D780
Panhumania (extract)	A A 5
	0 0 0
Educational Imprint 3485IST	5 1 4

As every child knows, the age of interstellar colonisation began in 3400 with the launch of the first great Colony Arks. The next two decades was a time of waiting. The Arks were predicted to make landfall twelve years into the new Millenium. The message that they would send once they arrived there should arrive back 4 years later. 3416 was the year which found humanity waiting for this message. When it did not come the prestige of the Quorumate tottered. People spoke angrily of the foolishness of the New Millenium Manifesto and eyes began turning once again inwards to the three homeworlds.

The message when it came was such an unlooked for reprieve that even a generation later people spoke of the attendant celebrations as the happiest times of their lives. The voices that a month before had called for the abolition of the Quorumate were raised in a tumult of adulation in its support. The men in the Quorumate that had been strongest in the support of sending the colony became overnight figures of legend.

In the next few years economic development leapt forward. The fervour for colonisation continued supported by the stream of messages from Tetaris that spoke of the continuing success of the colony there. The double ring of asteroids that lay between Xardil and Aractos was mined as never before. More Arks were built and eager citizens from every world vied with each other to be selected for the new colonies.

Four years later in 3420 the new Arks set off. Three each for the nearby stars Tuvis, Yardillia Minor and Zaphiri. The new Arks exploited the newly developed cryogenic technologies. For their passengers the long journeys would pass like a dream.

Because communications with the homeworlds took so much time centralised control was impossible. The Quorumate tried to maintain some influence over the colonies by sending carefully trained cadres of Nexus personnel with the Arks.

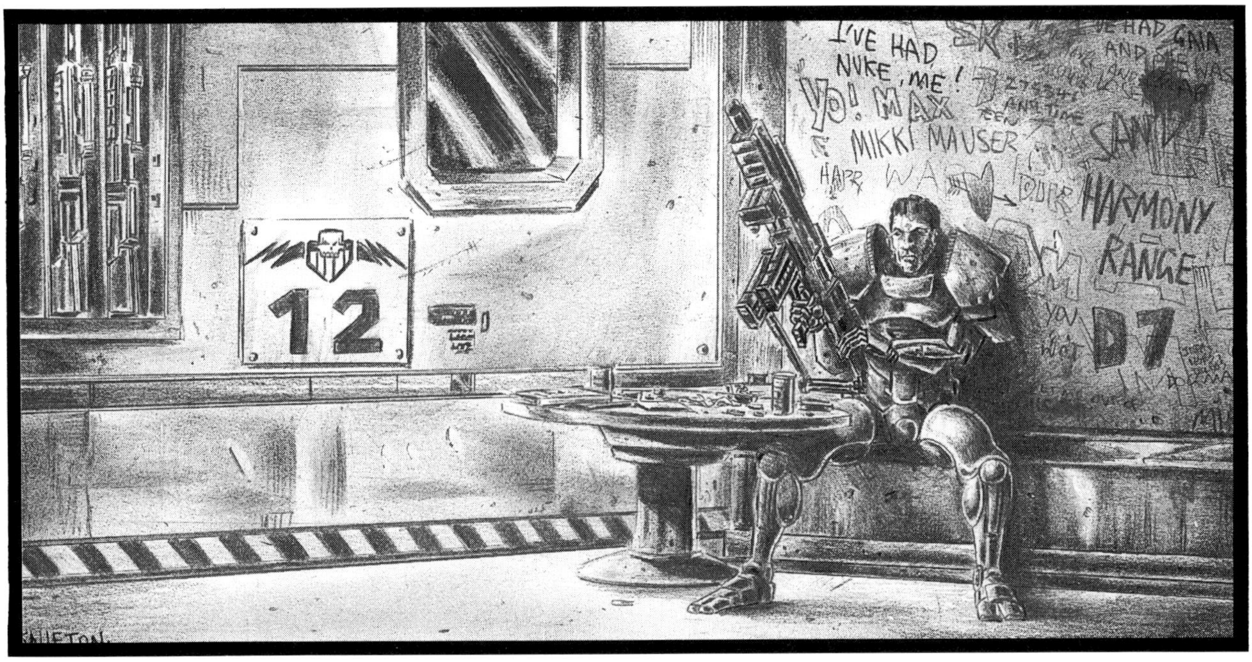

In 3438 the Pandaris Prime corporation invoked widespread disbelief when it announced that it had managed to find a way of transmitting signals at faster than light speeds. This was done by 'folding space' so that two points in spacetime that were at some distance[16] from each other were made to 'touch'.

To demonstrate this discovery Pandaris Prime proposed to receive a message 'instantaneously' from Tetaris IV four light years away. The homeworlds were astounded when a vague but discernible image was broadcast live on vidi-net that was claimed to come directly from Tetaris. When this signal was declared by the Quorumate to be genuine the news was received everywhere with stunned silence. In the next few months the colony on Tuvis came on air. The quality of the signal had increased markedly. It took some time for people to realise that they could now be in near immediate communication with their impossibly distant colonies.

16 these distances having a practical limit around 5-6 light years -

The political repercussions of this new technology were gigantic. For an enormous fee Pandaris Prime made the new Trans-Dimensional Carrier system available to the Quorumate.

Three years later Hajunka, a huge industrial giant, astounded the worlds when it announced that it had leased the TDC technologies from Pandaris Prime, made its own developments and had now managed to transport a physical entity instantaneously into the Tetaris System[17]. It demonstrated this to a sceptical audience by sending a probe there. Its arrival was confirmed by observers on Tetaris IV via TDC. A year later an animal had made the journey and soon after that

17 in fact this was close to the practical limits of the technology - for example, a 8 light year 'jump' would require space-folding equipment the size of a small moon and correspondingly enormous amounts of energy.

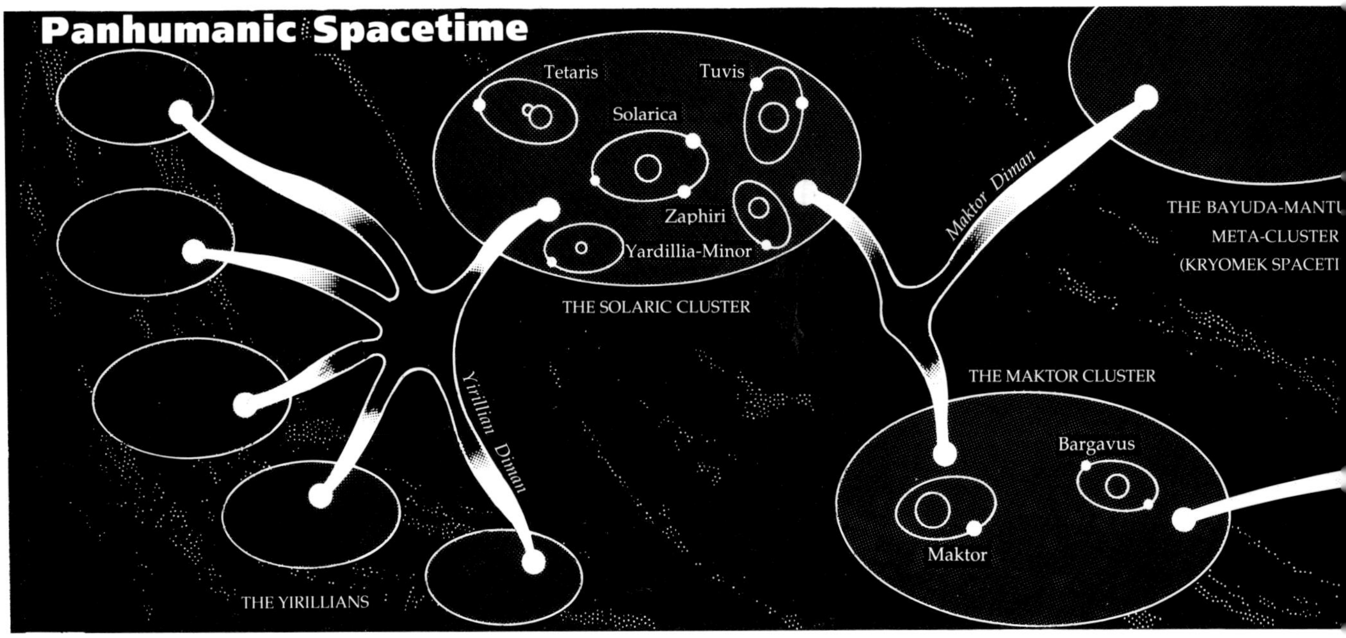

Irell Dayas became the first man to make a trans-dimensional jump between two star systems. With this the principal of trans-dimensional transportation had become a reality.

Within a few years huge freighters and colonist transporters were using the new space-folding equipment to make instantaneous voyages between the homeworlds and its colonies.

The forties and fifties saw a vast increase in planetary colonisation. The new trans-dimensional spaceships allowed panhumanic space to expand at an unprecedented rate.

In 3463 the Quorumate announced the Great Push in an attempt to control and reduce the level of anarchy that prevailed in the colonisation process. One of its main aims was to organise existing colonies and manage the planting of new ones.

Hajunka and Pandaris Prime heralded in a new age when they developed systems to exploit a trans-dimensional structure called a dimensional manifold. Up until this time these structures had been merely an interesting and obscure concept in trans-dimensional mathematics.

The new developments opened up vast new areas for colonisation. The dimensional manifolds connected humanity to portions of spacetime that were as much as ten thousand parsecs away, regions completely inaccessible before.

Several dimensional manifolds were discovered and each of these allowed access to new virgin stars clusters.

The first of these to be explored was the Maktor Cluster. At around the same time the Yirillian Diman was discovered and a colonising fleet was sent to the Yirillian Clusters. The discovery of the Trans-Maktorian Meta-Diman (Krellian Diman) opened up the countless worlds of the gargantuan Krellian Ring.

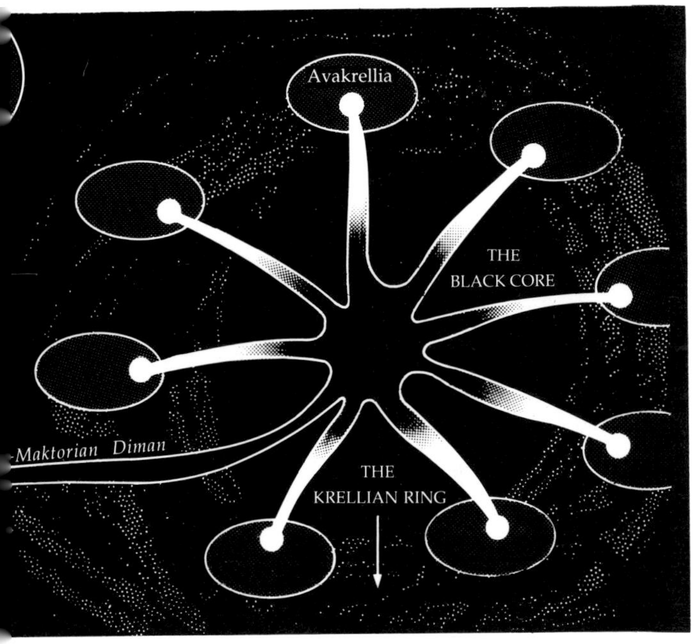

It was at this time that the process began where disaffected members of the panhumanic community took refuge in the Blackcore, the vast region of spacetime that lay within the Ring.

The Planetary Transmutation of Avakrellia II

Article Appearing in a Maktorian holomag
10.01.3479 IST

ALIS D377.79
2 7 0
0 1 1
2 0 1

The Kronos drifted like a vast, dark fish through a black ocean. Its hull was etched with the twisting tendrils and parabolas of coruscating light that were the telltale sign that it had just slipped through the trans-dimensional nothingness of a manifold. The glittering curves on its sides flashed ever more faintly as the gravitational eddies abated. Once spacetime was once again smooth there was nothing to indicate that the vast ship had moments before been eight parsecs away.

Somewhere deep inside the Kronos navigational computations flashed through its compcore. Ponderously it swung too pointing its nose towards a small star. Slowly it changed shape, pulling itself from a tight ellipsoid into something altogether more sleek. Here and there rods pushed out from its sides sprouting solgens[18] like leaves. Countless spots started glowing on the flat plates that formed the rear portion of its tail. The spots grew brighter - joined together and suddenly flared. The plates were now like suns spitting their own solar wind and forcing the Kronos forward.

---

18 solar generators.

KRONOS

In the homecore[19] faint cold lamps gleamed like underwater light through thick ice. Nothing moved. There were twelve biotrans modules[20] like coffins arranged along the deck. Each had a window of glass paler than the plastolene of the casing. A faint mist had formed on the glass. Inside dim shadows indicated the crew of the Kronos. There were seven men. The APT[21] called them "Planetary Transmutational Engineers". They called themselves Transmutes and were proud of it. As far as they were concerned their job was not unlike that of God's - they too made Edens in the wilderness.

The Kronos drifted silently towards the star for two months. The local diman opening from which they had come was unusually close to the Avakrellian system. A trans-dimensional jump would have used up a lot of the ship's precious energy reserves.

When the compcore brought the transmutes back to consciousness they found that the Kronos was already orbiting Avakrellia II. They did not hurry anything. Biotrans cryogenics was all good and well but it could not stop your limbs getting stiff on a long trip. They had been in stasis for five months already before they made the jump through the Trans-Maktorian Diman.

They got used to being human again. They ate and talked and played mentagames with the compcore. Some would spend hours staring down at the planet. It was orange now but would become turquoise within a few short years. Others, the more philosophical among them, wondered at this new world and what the galaxy would be losing. Even these shrugged - business is business. APT tried very hard to avoid selecting dreamers for its crews.

Then it began. Each of the men sat in his particular visideck. The compcore was programmed to take the Kronos along a standard Mollweide trajectory so that every micron of the planet would be covered. The visidecks swung out on long cantilevered arms through the hull and then out still further. It had been found out by experience that when one was transmuting a planet, it was safer to be out on a limb. Each of the visidecks had a biotrans capsule and had its own propulsion system. Each was capable of drifting free - for years if need be until rescuers would come drawn by its distress beacons. Each visideck was fitted with different sensors - each equipped according to it's transmute's function.

The Transmutor keyed in the release sequence. The Co-Transmutor confirmed it. The Kronos shuddered into life. There was a rumbling in its

belly that could be felt even in the visidecks. Green lights came on under each man's hand. Each transmute's systems were enabled and ready to go. The Kronos reached the alpha-point of the Mollweide trajectory and all hell broke loose.

The belly of the Kronos burst as if it were giving birth. A thin stream of helical descent capsules was paid out so that the Kronos seemed to be a vast spider passing across the planet the first thread of a web. Clusters of stratocombs fell, burst apart and then each sub-cluster burst apart again. Arcs of core-nodules were sown across the sky below. As the helical descent capsules struck the atmosphere they lit like fireflies. Their ceramic cases were protecting their delicate cargoes as they needled through the stratosphere. As the stratocombs hit the atmosphere in their turn they exploded with a blue flash. The fragments would fall through the atmosphere and draw out various harmful trace gases and strange poisonous compounds.

Three hours later the process was still continuing. Only 17.6% of Avakrellia II had been seeded. The light show was beautiful and continuous. The three RAGEM (Reproductive Atmospheric Gas Exchanging Modules) experts monitored the capsules as they spiralled down through the atmosphere. They attempted to guide them to land in favourable spots. When they landed the ceramic case fractured and spewed out a host of repropods. Each one of these analysed its surroundings and sent back data.

Avakrellia II was seeded. The Mollweide trajectory was repeated twice more. All the data from the repropods was checked and rechecked. They had it all. Everything was in place and ready. The planet was carpeted in the transmuting devices.

Kronos slipped smoothly into a loose orbit and then for the next few days the transmutes communed with the compcore. Circuits that had lain dormant for more than a year came alive. Correlation and optimisation of all the data must be

19 common name for the living quarters on huge vessels.

20 see "Biotran Cryogenics".

21 Agency for Planetary Transmutation

carried out. The repropods must be grouped and regrouped into dominant clusters and efficient flows of control must be determined. The computations required were astronomical and impossible without the aid of human intuitions.

Finally, and for the last time, the Kronos went into a Mollweide trajectory and the transmutes primed each of the repropods so that it knew its position in the scheme of things and its function. Finally a particular procedure of gas exchange was initiated.

Even though they could not see it the transmutes could almost feel it. They could feel the repropods burrowing down into the planet. Others thrust tubes into the air. Slowly they began to absorb gases from the air and extract minerals from the earth. Slowly they grew as they would do so for decades. Creating more of themselves. Spreading like a carpet of vegetation across the entire planet.

The philosophers in the Kronos remained behind to stare at the orange planet that soon would be blue. Then they too joined their comrades in their biotrans modules and fell into cryogenic sleep.

The Kronos swung round ponderously and pointed its nose towards a small star. Below, on the planet, the tiny machines laboured indefatigably. **They were making Eden.**

CHAPTER 5

Biotic Cryogenics

Entry in the Encyclopaedia Irallica	ALIS ED472
	4 4 1
	1 0 0
Encubed Imprint 3490 (Visicube 28.1.s099)	1 A 4

The transformation of biotic cryogenics into an important field of physical science occurred primarily between 3416 and 3420. This was essentially a consequence of the enthusiasm that was generated by the successful planting of the first interstellar colony on Tetaris IV. The discipline reached the zenith of its popularity in the 20s and 30s with the building of the second generation Colony Arks. At this time work was concentrated on maintaining large numbers of people in stable cryogenic suspension for periods of years that often stretched into decades.

The invention of spacefolding technologies and then of diman transportation brought an end to the massive cryogenic ark-banks and heralded in a new era of development. It was at this time the field split into the two different disciplines of biotrans cryogenics and biostatic cryogenics.

Nexus Technology

Biotrans Cryogenics

Entry in the Encyclopaedia Irallica

ALIS ED472.7
6 6 1
1 0 0
3 F 5

Encubed Imprint 3490
(Visicube 03.8.b223)

Biotrans cryogenics is a development of the biotransporting technologies employed in the Colony Arks. Used primarily by voyagers in deep space it is a refinement of earlier work which allows comfortable and accurate reductions in metabolic rate to be maintained. Cheap but sophisticated systems allow travellers to slip in and out of consciousness as easily as if the device were nothing more than an alarm clock. These systems have proliferated particularly in areas which are so distant from regular trans-dimensional routes that cryogenically assisted transportation is the only other viable option. More than 89% of journeys between cryo-adjacent worlds are now carried out using a biotrans system.

Application of Biostatic Cryogenic Systems to High Velocity Personnel Deployment Systems

Report presented to the Nexus Military Quorumate by the DBCR

ALIS AB472.98
1 6 8
3 0 0
1 F 8

DBCR_SR22245/Dept 5.3/5.5.3492

This department is currently exploring the possibility of grafting transient biostatic cryogenic control systems to two new high velocity Personnel Deployment Systems (PDS).

Both PDS are considered highly promising developments but are currently unusable because of the high degrees of biosystemic stress that is imposed on the operative.

The two systems being examined are the Helical Planetary Descent Capsule System (HePDeCS) and the Ballistic Delivery System (BaDS).

The first consists of a personnel capsule suspended from a fixed ablation resistive rotorwing assembly. The capsule is formed of a double shell of heat resistant iridio-ceramic and contains a low yield life-support system. Its intended use is to allow personnel to be 'dropped' directly from supra-stratospheric craft through the atmosphere and to deploy them accurately on the planet surface.

The trajectory from the launch craft is conditioned to allow a shallow rate of descent. The ceramic shell easily resists atmospheric ablation. The rotorwing is folded behind the capsule and is protected within the confines of its jet stream. On reaching the troposphere the capsule assumes a vertical orientation and the rotorwing is automatically deployed. This immediately causes the capsule to spin around its vertical axis. This motion reduces the vertical velocity of the capsule. The shock absorbing system severely reduces any impact damage.

In experimental drops all subjects were well sustained by the life-support systems. Minimal somatic damage occurred. Metabolic and psychological integrity were however completely upset. Subjects were rendered unconscious and unable even to activate the release levers that open the ceramic capsule. The main cause of this is of course the rotation of the capsule which reaches a rate of 120rpm.

The Ballistic Delivery System is a battlefield PDS that is intended to propel personnel deep into and sometimes behind enemy lines. (The expensive nature of the technology precludes its use except in tactically high yield scenarios.)

The subject is fired in a ballistic capsule. Each capsule is provided with a means of ground at-

tachment which is specific to the local terrain. The velocity of projection is necessarily high and the capsule on landing explodes open. The geometry of this explosion is carefully aligned to a concentric-shell blast and does not cause any damage to the subject. It simultaneously releases the subject and provides a certain amount of stun-cover.

In experiments all subjects suffered severe mental and metabolic disruption. In fact, very few subjects were able to remain conscious beyond the point of impact.

Obviously two separate approaches might be adopted to reduce the biosystemic disruption in both systems. The first would be to modify the operating parameters of the systems themselves, the second to modify the subject so that he was capable of resisting it.

The former approach is unlikely to succeed[22] because the operating parameters of each system are already being pushed to the limits. The latter, which represents our approach is showing promise. Biostatic cryogenic modules have been added to both capsules. These record the metabolic and mental state of the subject as he is strapped into the capsule. In flight the modules reduce the subject to a condition of stasis where he experiences little metabolic and mental activity. The module is tuned in to the impact absorbing equipment and carefully controls the smooth resuscitation of both metabolic and mental activity to match the recorded profiles as closely as possible.

Experiments so far carried out have managed to reduce the biosystemic stress to manageable levels and better results are too be expected soon. Subjects exited the capsule suffering only mild nausea and in the case of the Descent Capsule a certain amount of residual 'dizziness'.

The Development of Battlefield Striders

ALIS CD364.71

Entry in the Encyclopaedia Irallica

0 1 3
0 0 0
0 0 1

Encubed Imprint 3490 (Visicube 30.9.g565)

Bipedal battlefield chassis are the natural conclusion to a long tradition of mobile weapon platforms which can carry heavier armaments than a human infantryman.

Previous design solutions were essentially wheeled though the wheels might be enhanced and protected by tracks of various sorts. These cer-

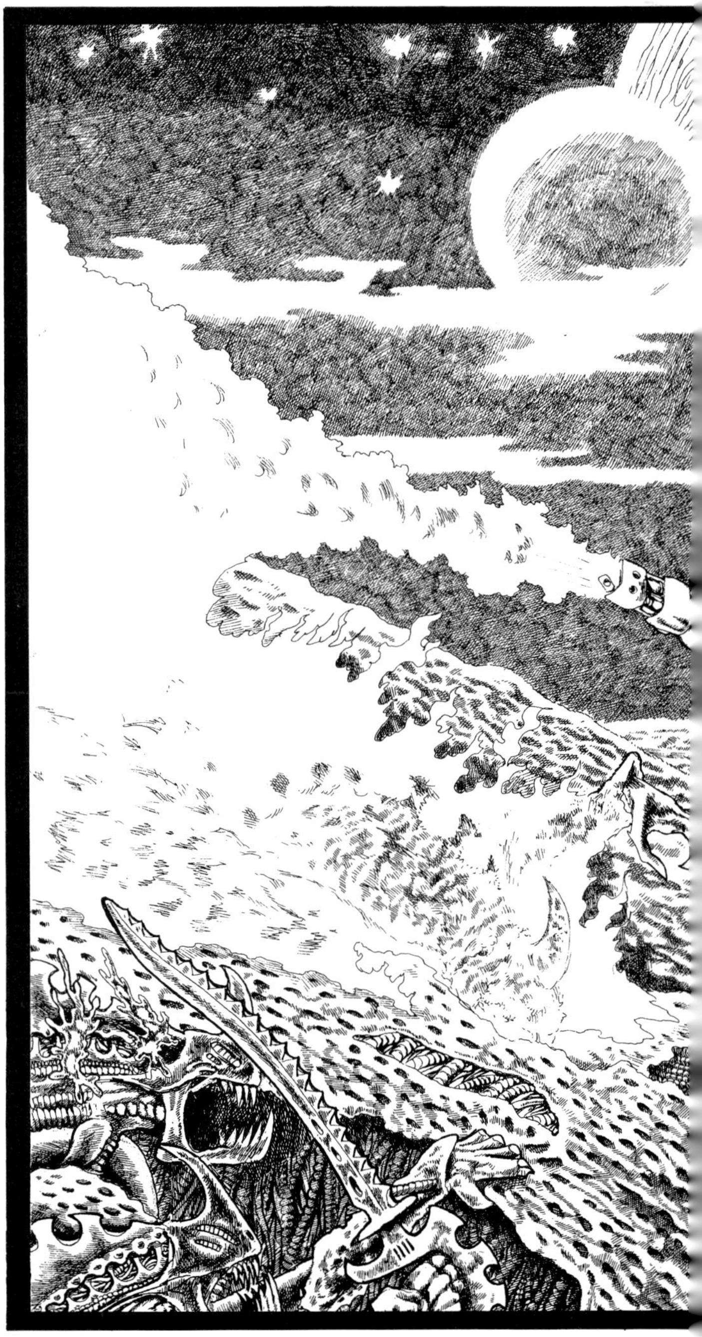

[22] this is not entirely true. Modifications were made to the HepDeCS by giving the capsule a double shell which forms a roto-buffering sandwich containing a nano-polymerized gel with a temperature related velocity gradient. Similar use was made of this compound in the design of the BaDS impact absorbing equipment.

tainly extended the possible range of terrains for which the vehicle might be considered suitable. However all such solutions suffer from being to some extent terrain specific or even of being ineffective in many terrain types.

Various hovering technologies have been developed which provide solutions to most of these problems. They do however have the great disadvantage that they are a high energy cost solution which can often lead to a compromise in the operative range of the vehicle.

The bipedal solution provides the flexibility which allows the vehicle to handle most terrain types well. A dynamically balanced bipedal vehicle finds stable equilibrium at rest and has a smooth profile in motion - making it an excellent weapons platform. There is additionally an obvious and natural affinity to the mode of locomotion of the human infantryman which produces an important synergy on the battlefield.

23 the Ksirus "Helcat".

Battlefield Cybernetics

by Eyagada Bibarina-Tlesh

Article Appearing in Scientific Xardillian

(Extract) Decarax 3492 IST

ALIS D359.3
2 2 6
2 0 1
0 1 1

Cybernetic systems have been operating on the battlefield for centuries. Most weapons systems will incorporate at least some cybernetic technology. However it is only in the last few years that stand alone cybernetic warrior modules have been seeing active battle service.

The first of these units were small cyberized versions of contemporary battlefield walkers[23]. Many are still in service and are useful as expendable frontal assault weapons.

These new classes of cybernetic warriors have been made possible by advances in cyberneural engineering and particularly the Active Cyberneural Matrix (ACM) developed by the

Agarax Corporation. These developments were partially financed by the Nexus Quorumate.

The development of these weapons was a response to lessons learnt on the battlefield during the Hivestone Incursion Crisis: it was necessary to create a frontline battlefield unit that could withstand full frontal assault by the Kryomek.

The Talos Series Battlefield Unit

Pre-battle briefing for Nexus personnel to acclimatise them to cyborg units	ALIS AD359.397 2 2 A 4 0 1 1 1 4
07.07.3490 IST	

The Talos series comprises a system of interchangeable modules that allow a variety of cybernetic combat units to be purpose-assembled for a given battlefield.

The basic chassis of the Talos Series Battlefield Unit is analogous to the human endoskeleton. It is made of an iridio-steel alloy interlaced with crystallated ceramic filaments. This is bonded to a core which is a magno-shielding sponge with conducting micro-channels. The structure of this sponge allows for auto-rechannelling in cases of anything other than the most severe impact trauma. This reduces the likelihood of component systems becoming cybertronically isolated.

Atomically welded to this endoskeleton are a number of units each encased in a shell of beryllium-bronze which has a nano-gauge single-molecule mesh embedded as a surface feature. The addition of the mesh was made necessary to help counter the effects of the Kryomek single-molecule blade which sliced through the earlier models with little resistance. Additionally the surface is coated in an active bioneutralizing film that will counter some if not all Kryomek biocorrosives.

Articulation of the Talos Unit is modelled closely on the human pattern. Motive power is provided by two high-yield fusion reactors. Each is capable of powering the unit independently. The torque produced by the reactors is transmitted into motion by magnocoupled disc and ball joints which have a very high detente torque.

The Talos Unit may be fitted with a variety of fully integrated arm-weapon modules. This module replaces the left arm. The right arm is humano-articulated to match standard human grip indices and will take any standard issue hand weapon.

The unit is a general weapon carrying chassis and does have the facilities for attaching a number of other weapons. These include other specialised somato-prostheses[24] such as an integrated head-weapon module.

Tactical delimiters indicate that the unit is best used as a frontal assault weapon. Its strengths are its greater resistance and relentless aggression which are coupled with no self-preservation restrictions. Its main weakness is a consequence of its strength - it is incapable of the flexible response of human personnel.

24 artificial body replacements

visicube 6-BR/5 - [07:05:55] 01/01/3492 IST
operation code: M273.92 DD07/CM1-C01-S01
location: Hive - Karanada-Omicron - Bayuda-Man. 004
subject: [Ksirus Hellcat] - hive - Kryomek Warriors

CHAPTER 6

A Survey of Kryomek Science

Report presented to the Nexus Military Quorumate by the NCSS

NCSS_SR17534/CC X5/12.4.3491

ALIS	A587.5	
1	2	A
4	1	1
1	9	4

There are many aspects of Kryomek science that present a great contrast with our own. It is evident that the origins of their science lie in the meticulous management of resources which a Hive system represents. More interesting is the fact that their natural bias for bio-genetic engineering has resulted in the development of technologies which differ so greatly from our own. A simple demonstration of this can be obtained by making a direct comparison between some of our military technology and some of theirs. Human weaponry is essentially based on three complementary systems that of particle beam, MASER and other energy weapons, that of gauss weapons and that of explosives. In contrast, Kryomek weapons are of an entirely chemical and bio-mechanical nature. They make extensive use of powerful bio-corrosives, highly engineered contact poisons and a variety of very sophisticated chemical energy systems. This is complemented by extensive modifications of living forms through synthetico-mechanical splicing, various kinds of assemblo-biomass plastication and all kinds of synthobiogenetic implantation.

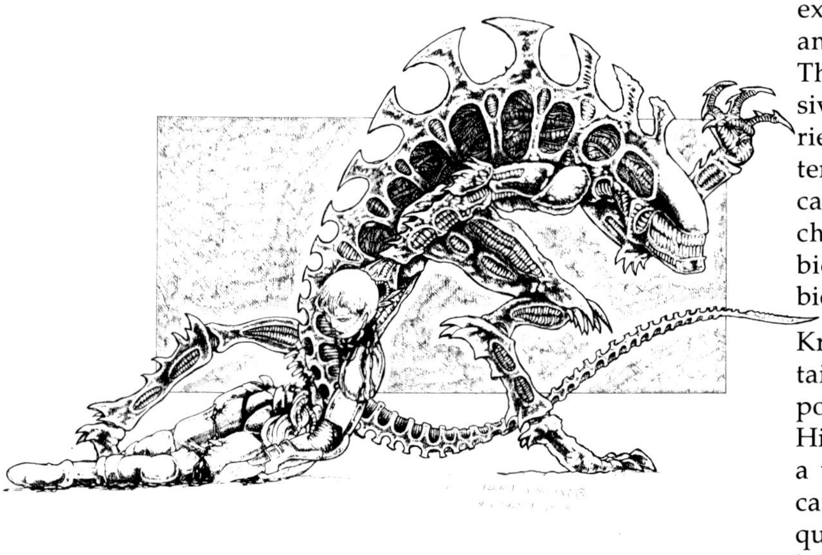

Kryomek science owes much of its success to certain inbuilt characteristics of the humblest components of the Hive Meta-System - that is the Hivebrood (this generic name is now used to cover a wide range of quite distinct modified 'worker caste' Kryomek). Paramount amongst these is a quality derived from the hivebrood's function of labouring endlessly on the maintenance of the hive. Over time some specialisation set in which led to this ability being amplified many times so

Kryomek Bio-Technology

that castes of creatures evolved from the hivebrood to perform tasks that amongst humanity are performed by scientists.

In its present form this has achieved a high degree of sophistication where a hierarchy of Hivebrood operate under the direct chemical control of the Hivemaster constantly modifying and improving the hive and all its systems. It seems to be certain now that each Great Hive has its own completely independent 'science' (this explains why there is so much variation in spacecraft design, weaponry etc. between one Great Hive and another). There is no standardisation as with our technologies. Instead everything is continuously redesigned according to any new data that reaches the Hivemaster. Neither is there anything that we would call cybernetics. Instead control systems are derived from organic sources, nervous systems are removed from living creatures and imbedded in a bio-mechanical chassis. Even their computers have at their centre organic processing units that are often the brains of the organisms that they prey on - as often as not other Kryomek.

All in all the power and scope of Kryomek science poses a severe threat to our perceptions of what constitutes 'good science' and we are now locked into a technology race with the Kryomek whose ultimate winner is still to be determined.

Kryomek Weaponry

Report presented to the Nexus Military Quorumate by the NMI

ALIS AB587.46
1 2 8
4 1 1
1 9 4

NMI_SR22245/Dept 5.3/5.5.3492

All information concerning Kryomek battlefield technology has been obtained from two very different sources. The first is that collated from debriefing information - that is from the eye witness reports of NTFA personnel that have encountered this equipment in the field. This has largely been superseded by the second, more recent data that has been obtained from the careful scientific disassembly and analysis of those pieces of equipment that have been captured from the Kryomek.

The analysis of any equipment of Kryomek manufacture is always attended by a certain degree of danger. Our researchers are here dealing with technologies that often have no counterpart at all in our own science. Furthermore, these technologies are all technologies of destruction and are by their very nature highly unstable.

The first thing that can be safely said about all Kryomek equipment examined thus far is that it demonstrates a close synthesis between biogenetic engineering and more conventional electrograv-mechanics. This is one of the few generalities that can be made. The most startling thing about Kryomek technology is the lack of standardisation. It is this infinite variety that has plagued our researches from the beginning. The other great problem is that Kryomek systems are fused together imperceptibly - nothing has ever been isolated that could properly be called a component.

We are now certain that this equipment is in fact designed to fulfil different functional requirements on the battlefield - so that there are weapons that are clearly intended for anti-personnel use - while others are to be used to assault heavily armoured installations.

Anti-personnel weapons use exotic biogenetic technologies. Some launch biopod shells that disperse various kinds of virulent plasmogenetically engineered algoplasmid vectors. These are encased in high-gradient osmotic membranes that serve to allow them to quickly penetrate even 3 micra thick iridio-plasticated laminates. Initially these weapons were frighteningly effective against our ground troops - though developments in counter-gradial osmolaminates has redressed the balance somewhat.

Other anti-personnel weapons include spore launchers (that fire hyper-metabolic necrotropic mycelia encased in z3-condition resistant casings that have a wide q-dispersal range and impact to cause rapid pernicious mycelium infestation) and a bewildering variety of rapid impulse projectors that generally eject fluid or semi-fluid compounds some of which bear a striking resemblance to our own mucilated isoton-napalm.

Assault weapons also differ widely and are often also used against personnel. The most common use dynamically engineered bio-corrosives. Shells of irregular shapes (that, incidentally, when tested in computer fluid simulations were revealed to have remarkably low drag coefficients in all atmosphere types with visco-penetration parameters higher than 2523) are propelled by high yield biostatic reactions. The most singular property of these is that the initial bio-corrosive gradient is readjusted as each shell is fired and rapidly converges on an optimal corrosive profile. This has necessitated the NTFA to develop ever more complex nano-polymerized armour laminates - though these become obsolete from one battle to the next.

Recently a host of new heavy assault weapons have been unleashed that consist of critical blends of accelerated, hyper-metabolic genoclones that have the ability to penetrate and structurogranulate even the most resistant of our laminates (thus making them brittle and highly impact sensitive). Unless new materials are produced soon we will no longer have the capability to produce effective armour or to build defensible structures.

Carapace Armour

Report presented to the Nexus Military Quorumate by the NMI (Extract)	ALIS DB587.3862 1 3 A 1 2 1
NMI_SR22278/Dept 5.3/15.7.3492	1 E 6

Rather than develop artificial external battle armours the Kryomek chose to enhance their somatogenic chitinous carapaces.

Scrapings taken from Warrior Caste carapaces showed a bewildering variety of techniques had been employed in applying strengthening finishes. When analysed, a portion of recovered Warmaster carapace revealed that it had been successively covered by no less than an astounding 2000 separate layerings. Some layers had been applied as aerosolic sprays, while others even revealed the tell-tale feathering of brushwork. Single-molecule films had been finely interleaved over the whole surface and were bonded closely at a molecular level to present a complex shielding architecture. The whole was rubbed over with dense biopolymerized resins.

Under most test conditions the Warmaster carapace easily out-performed iridio-laminates and was found to be more resilient even than crystallated beryllium bronzes - especially to impact damage.

visicube 6-BR/17 - [11:08:07] 31/11/3491 IST
operation code: M273.71 DD06/SM7-C03-S7
location: Gamma-Hegada 2 - Bayuda-Man. 003
subject: [Kryomek Warrior] + [Single-Molecule Blade] - Gamma-Hegada - Gamma-Hegada 1 - <Battle for Gamma-Hegada 2>
analysis: six (6) centions of SWAT troops destroyed by Kryomek Swarm. Nexus troops encumbered by envirobattle armour & low gravity. Kryomek suffer no appreciable performance degradation. Surface of moon obliterated from the orbiting Dreadnought the Katar.

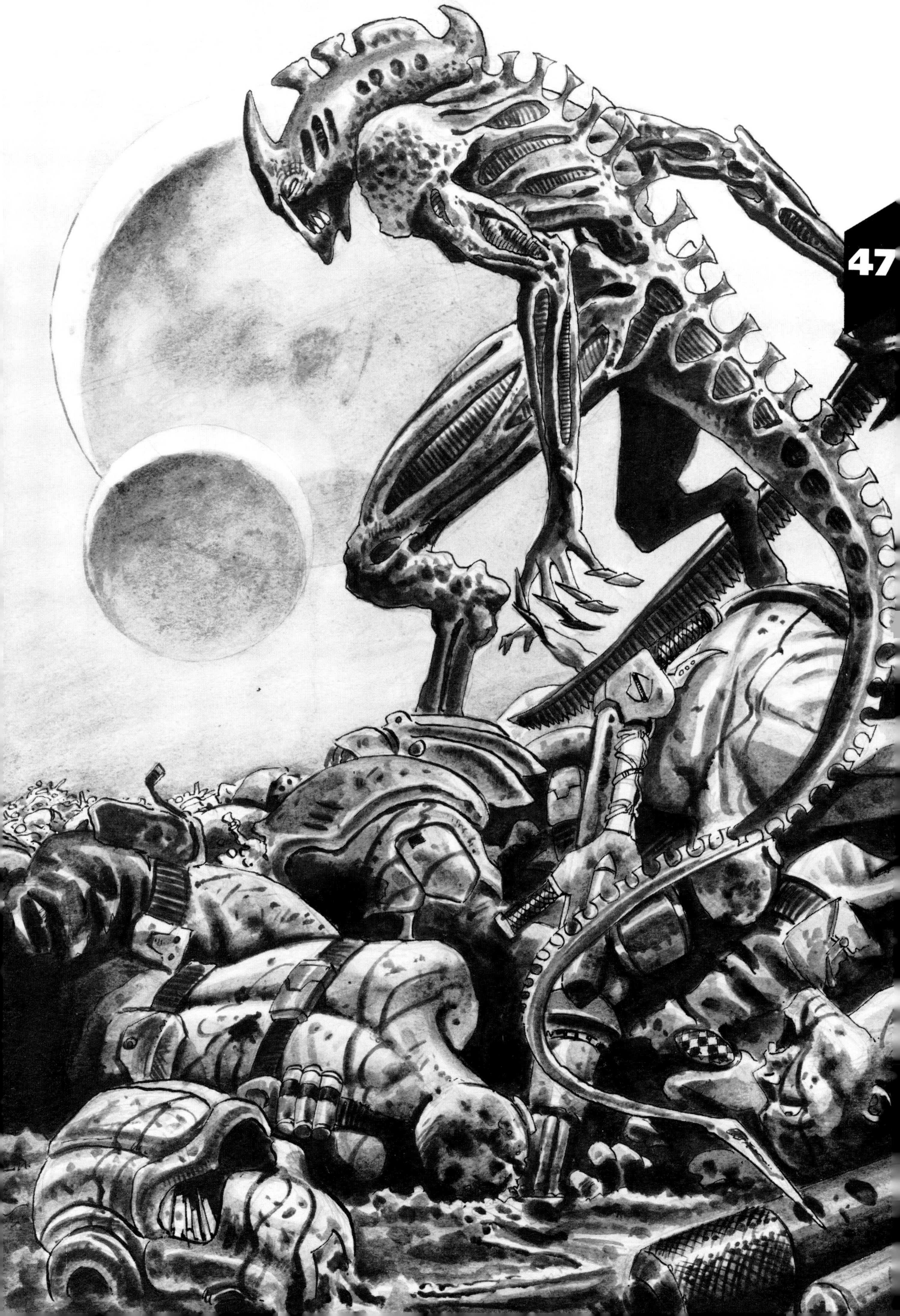

CHAPTER

7

As long as the Kryomek held the interstice at the other end of the diman they were powerless.

The Hivestone Incursion Crisis

Entry in the Encyclopaedia Irallica

Encubed Imprint 3490 (Visicube 24.4.t343)

ALIS C799.2
E A 3
1 2 0
5 1 9

The Hivestone appeared in the Maktor System on 22.04.3489 IST. It materialised near the interstice of the Maktor Diman. Its appearance was accompanied by a substantial perturbation in the spacetime continuum. The gravitational waves were detected as far away as Gamma-Bargavus 0.45 parsecs away. The first instruments to detect the intruder however were those of the freighter Sidonia which was heading for the interstice. The Sidonia was intending to use the Maktor Diman to jump to the Solarica Cluster.

The Sidonia's communications systems were almost swamped by the disturbance but its crew managed to send a visidata packet transmission to Tau-Maktor , the only inhabited planet in the system. There, Nexus personnel attempted an analysis of the data. They were unable to ascertain the nature of the disturbance beyond the fact that it seemed that it had something to do with the asteroid that had appeared near the interstice. They were however sufficiently concerned to attempt to send a Clearance 6 transmission to the Quorumate on Irallia. This could not be sent for 12 hours because the residual gravitational perturbations made use of the TDC impossible.

By the time the Quorumate received the message the Hivestone had begun to open. At its centre was a complete Kryomek hive. The Swarmfleet broke free of the Hivestone along shafts that had been solidly packed for passage through the diman. Within a few hours the TDC relay was destroyed.

It took sixteen days for the Swarmfleet to reach Tau-Maktor. The inhabitants had seen them coming but could do nothing to stop them. They

The Great Wars

were cut off from any help. The population of the planet was completely annihilated.

On Irallia the analysis of the last Tau-Maktorian transmission was still in its initial stages when the TDC relay went dead. The Quorumate became concerned when the relay did not come back on line for several hours. There were too many back-up systems for it to be merely a systems failure.

As the period of TDC silence stretched out into days the military throughout the Solaric Cluster were put on yellow alert.

Five days later the diman dreadnought Nemesis set off for the Maktor Diman interstice in the Zaphiri System. The Nemesis reached it fifteen days later and made the jump on schedule to the Maktor System.

The Kryomek had had time to make preparations. As the Nemesis materialised out of the diman the Kryomek attacked. The dreadnought was still suffering from the systemic degradation that accompanies diman jumps and was quickly overwhelmed.

Panic spread through the Solaric Cluster. The way was open for the Kryomek to invade through the Maktorian diman. They did not come.

There was some relief when the expected invasion did not materialise but, on the other hand,

the loss of the Nemesis made it obvious that the Quorumate was cut off from the Maktor Cluster . The dreadnought had managed to make some TDC transmissions in the early part of the battle so that the Quorumate had some idea what they were up against. In spite of this they could do nothing. As long as the Kryomek held the interstice at the other end of the diman they were powerless. Panhumanic spacetime was effectively split in two.

Meanwhile, the planets in the Krellian Ring were completely aware of what was going on in the Maktor Cluster. The TDC relay at the Bargavus interstice of the Trans-Maktorian Diman was still completely intact. The Nexus authorities on each planet tried desperately to contact the Quorumate but the TDC link back to Solarica was broken.

Finally an Emergency Quorumate was set up on the planet Heptor and began to make preparations to invade the Maktor Cluster. Everyday that passed saw the panic increasing as the news leaked out and spread around the Ring. People knew that the Bargavus interstice was an open door to the Kryomek through which they could reach any of their worlds. After all the interstice was less than 2 light years away from the Swarmfleet. Many abandoned their planets and fled into the Blackcore.

The military did not have the resources to quell the disturbances and the Ring worlds fell into ever greater anarchy.

Before everything was ready the Emergency Quorumate received intelligence reports indicating that the Kryomek Swarmfleet had made a transdimensional jump into the Bargavus System and thus towards the opening to the Trans-Maktor Diman. Thinking that the Kryomek were moving to invade the Ring, the invasion force, even though it was unready, was immediately dispatched to intercept them - preferably in the Maktor Cluster before they came through the diman.

The three Leviathan class dreadnoughts, the Shiva, the Baal and the Astarte, materialised in the Bargavus System and managed to deploy their weapons systems without any interference from the Kryomek. The Kryomek Swarmfleet retreated before them and jumped back into the Maktor System. The human fleet could do nothing but follow. It was essential to contain the contagion before it infected other systems in the Maktor Cluster.

The Swarmfleet retired before them moving rapidly towards Tau-Maktor. The battle was fought three days later in orbit around the planet. The Swarmfleet was reinforced by forces coming up from the planet. It came to meet them and engaged the human fleet in apparent disorder.

The battle was long. The Astarte and a huge volume of space was completely annihilated by a transient black hole when a Kryomek boarding party managed to access her spacefolding equipment and energise it with an unstable configuration. The Baal was riddled with Kryomek and most of its crew were annihilated. The Shiva managed to vaporise a large portion of the Swarm Fleet and the Astarte implosion took out most of the rest. Thousands of Kryomek deserted the smouldering wrecks of their ships and fell burning like stars into the planets atmosphere.[25]

Support craft completed the destruction of the Swarmfleet but it took several days for marines and SWAT teams to clear the Baal. A pocket of the original ship's crew survived though many of them were driven insane by their experiences.

Though the fleet was severely mauled it limped its way into Tau-Maktor orbit. It was thought unlikely that the Kryomek would have any forces left capable of assaulting a dreadnought in suprastratospheric[26] space.

Scans of the surface made it obvious that the planet was completely devastated. The Kryomek processes of bioregenesis were already well under way. Besides this, with astonishing speed, the Kryomek hivebrood had been at work building a hive.

---

25 Amazingly it was later ascertained that many of these survived by being contained in some kind of ablative shell.

26 in space - beyond the atmosphere

A Planetary Stratecom was dispatched to the planet surface to attack the hive with a four myriads of marines and one of convicts. At first the Kryomek showed little resistance but then a Swarm sallied out of the partially completed hive and attacked the Nexus forces. These had to retire before the punishing assault.

The myriads were drawn back bloodied into the Shiva and the Baal. Urgent requests were sent back to the Emergency Quorumate on Heptor. The message came back.

"We cannot hazard our troops against the hive on Tau-Maktor . But neither can we leave the hive to grow to maturity. To act is folly. Not to act is folly. There is only one option.....

Burn Tau-Maktor !"

And so it was. The Shiva and the crippled Baal poured nucleonic fire down upon the planet. Tau-Maktor burned.

A single myriad of convict troops was sent down in isolation suits. They approached the melted ruins of the Hive expecting it to be an empty shell and found it full of Kryomek. After the battle the myriad was reorganised and there were barely enough men to make up four centions.

A transmission arrived from Heptor that was the counsel of despair. It handed all decisions in the Maktor Cluster theatre over to the fleet commanders. In desperation the stratecoms gathered for conference in the Shiva. It was decided that the Shiva and all fully operational vessels should move off to attack the Hivestone since it seemed to be the source of the invasion. The Baal and the other ships would remain behind in orbit around Tau-Maktor. The stratecoms both feared that the Hivestone might move into another system in the cluster and hoped that they might be able to destroy the Kryomek at the source of the infestation.

The Shiva approached the Hivestone not knowing what to expect. It seemed completely inert.

Attempts were made to blast the asteroid with nucleonics. The outer surface was fragmented but instruments indicated that the hive itself remained intact. Other attempts were made to drop high yield cobalt fission devices down the shafts but these were defeated by the shaft architecture and exploded near the surface.

At last the stratecoms gave their assent to a troop assault. Their first objective was to secure a foothold on the Hivestone. This was achieved against fierce opposition from the Kryomek. The next move was an all out assault from the foothold.

First all the convict myriads were committed. They took fearful casualties but managed to penetrate some distance down into the Hivestone. When those units had been exhausted a specially modified nucleonic device was detonated at the deepest point reached.

The marines went in as the second wave of the assault. The stratecoms learnt early on that the Kryomek seemed to react to them as if they were a single organism. A hope arose that at the centre of the Hivestone there might be a single directing intelligence.[27] The Hivestone might have an Achilles Heel. The attack was mounted with redoubled intensity.

Finally the marines were so mauled that they too had to be pulled out. The stratecoms played their final card. The SWAT teams were sent down the shaft. Though there were fewer and fewer Kryomek encountered these fought with ever increasing ferocity.

At last the troopers broke through the defenders and penetrated the hivecore. Specially trained convict suicide squads were sent in. Inside they encountered for the first time a Hivemaster. It was evacuated but the troopers were carrying thermonucleonic pulse devices. The blast fused the hive to the molten rock of the asteroid.

Almost imperceptibly the surviving Kryomek slowed down until they reached a state of almost complete inactivity. The asteroid was rigged for demolition. The Shiva retreated to a safe distance as the Hivestone was blasted to powder.

A message arrived from the Baal saying that the Kryomek opposition had suddenly collapsed on Tau-Maktor . The half finished hive there was demolished and all remaining Kryomek were ruthlessly exterminated.

It took several weeks more to make sure that every single bio-fragment of the Kryomek contagion was destroyed. Of course the nucleonics made sure that Tau-Maktor would be uninhabitable for centuries.

The TDC relay at the Maktor interstice was replaced and the two halves of panhumanic spacetime were once again united.

The Glindex Fork

by Yadis Maruganya

ALIS CD799.4

Entry in the Encyclopaedia Irallica

E A 3
A 2 1
7 1 8

06.07.3494 IST (to be encubed 3497)

In the aftermath of the Hivestone incursion the panhumanic society was left in disarray. The Nexus Quorumate had lost not only prestige but also two of its Leviathan dreadnoughts and an enormous number of casualties; the worlds of the Krellian Ring were to sink into five years of anarchy and confusion; and everyone trembled at the prospect that more Hivestones might appear in panhumanic spacetime.

27 Nothing was known at this time about Hivemasters.

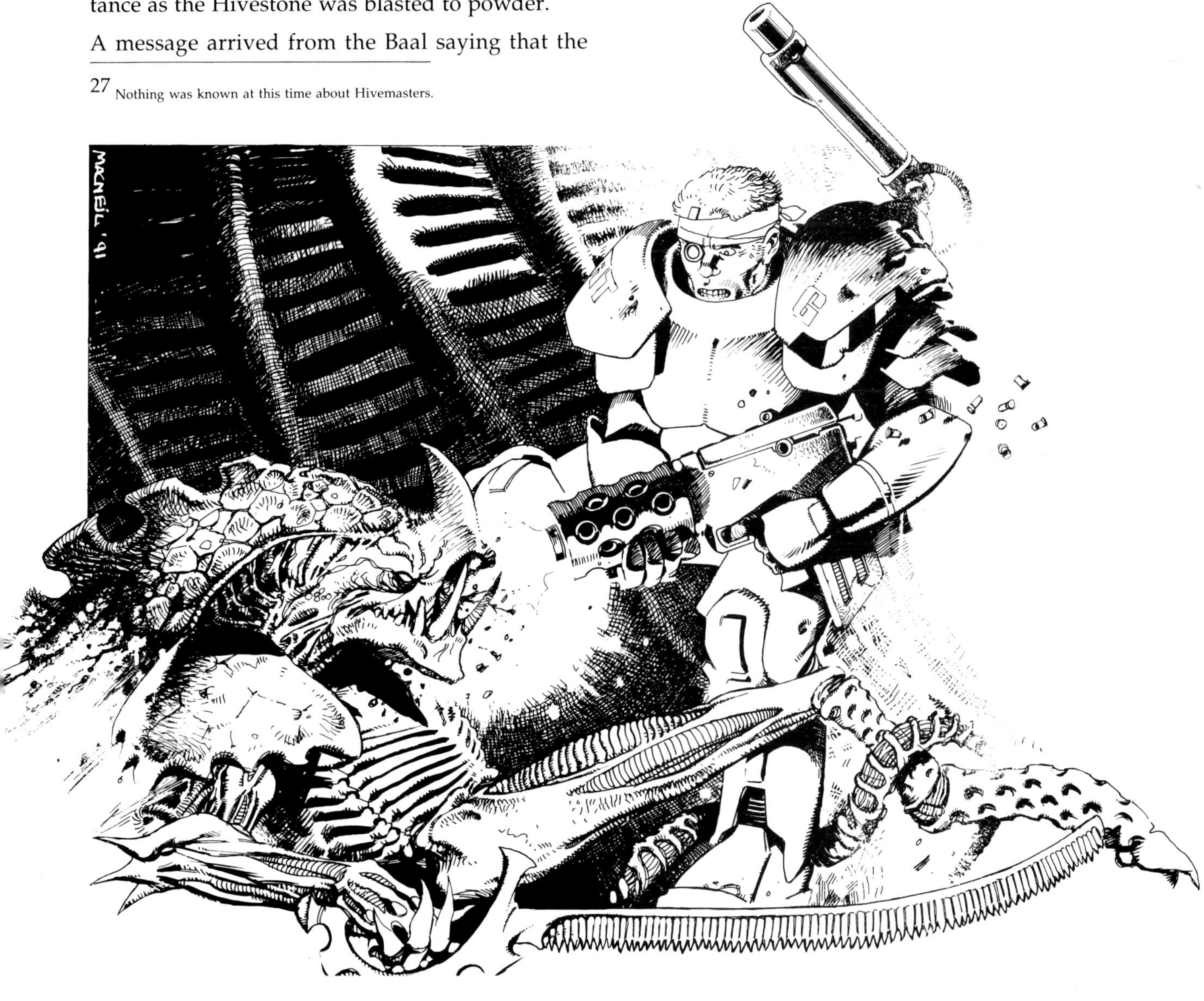

One man came forward at this time of crisis and thrilled humanity with his vision. His name was Tatuya Glindex and he was a Master Strategist and adviser to the Nexus Quorumate. He presented a deep analysis of the crisis. He also proposed a plan of such breadth and simplicity that at first his words were greeted with a stunned silence. This plan became known as the "Glindex Fork".

This plan rested on his analysis. He suggested a theory to explain the actions of the Kryomek. He argued that the way in which the Hivestone arrived in the Maktor system, the nature of the Hivestone itself and the fact that the Kryomek made no attempt to use either of the two dimensional manifolds to attack either the Solaric Cluster or the Krellian Ring pointed to one simple answer. The Kryomek had not mastered the probability mathematics necessary to locate the precise position of the diman interstices.

To the question of how it was that the Hivestone got there at all he answered by asking people to consider that the Hivestone had never demonstrated that it had any kind of motive power whatsoever. He stated that it was not a craft at all. In fact he produced a brilliantly argued polemic that demonstrated that using any conceivable energy source the Hivestone would have had to have huge - and very obvious - propulsion units.

His conclusion was that the Hivestone had been towed to the *neighbourhood* of the Maktor Diman interstice in Kryomek spacetime and then subjected to a vast implosion that tore an opening into the Diman. On visidata taken at the time he pointed out surface features on the Hivestone that might indicate that it had been vastly greater in size at some recent time. The depth at which the hive was buried in the asteroid might have been necessitated to safeguard it against the gravitational vortices generated by the clumsy method of entry into the Diman.

He postulated that the Kryomek were as yet unable even to locate the rough neighbourhood of an interstice - and perhaps could not even detect the presence of a diman at all. He argued that they may only have located the interstice in Kryomek spacetime because they followed Admiral Mankturian[28] back to it.

One of his most harrowing conclusions was that the arrival of the Hivestone in the Maktor Cluster was, in a manner of speaking, fortuitous. After all, if the Kryomek did not have the probability mathematics then it could have just as easily appeared in the Solaric Cluster. The disaster might then have been far greater.

He reminded people that nothing he was saying indicated that the Kryomek might not send more Hivestones.

He demonstrated with the help of a team of probability mathematicians from the megacorp Pandaris Prime that it was theoretically possible to close access to a diman from an associated interstice though this would take enormous quantities of energy. He proposed to annihilate the Maktor Diman Interstice in Kryomek spacetime and thus to deny the Kryomek access to panhumanic spacetime altogether.

His solution, the 'Glindex Fork' was based on the assumption that it was unlikely that the Kryomek would not have fortified the Interstice and that to jump the task force through to it would be suicidal.

Instead he produced a visicube which he had obtained from Pandaris Prime which showed a number of new diman openings that had as yet been unexplored. Amongst these he indicated one which lay on an otherwise useless diman one end of which was near an obscure world on the Krellian Ring , the other which lay within 0.62 parsecs of the target interstice.

His plan was to send a vast armada through this diman, approach the target interstice from the rear and attempting to obliterate the Kryomek presence there hold the system long enough to allow the Interstice to be closed.

---

28 see "The disaster at Aleph-Jang'ada III re-examined".

The Glindex Fork

The Bayuda Interstice on the Maktor Diman must be closed!

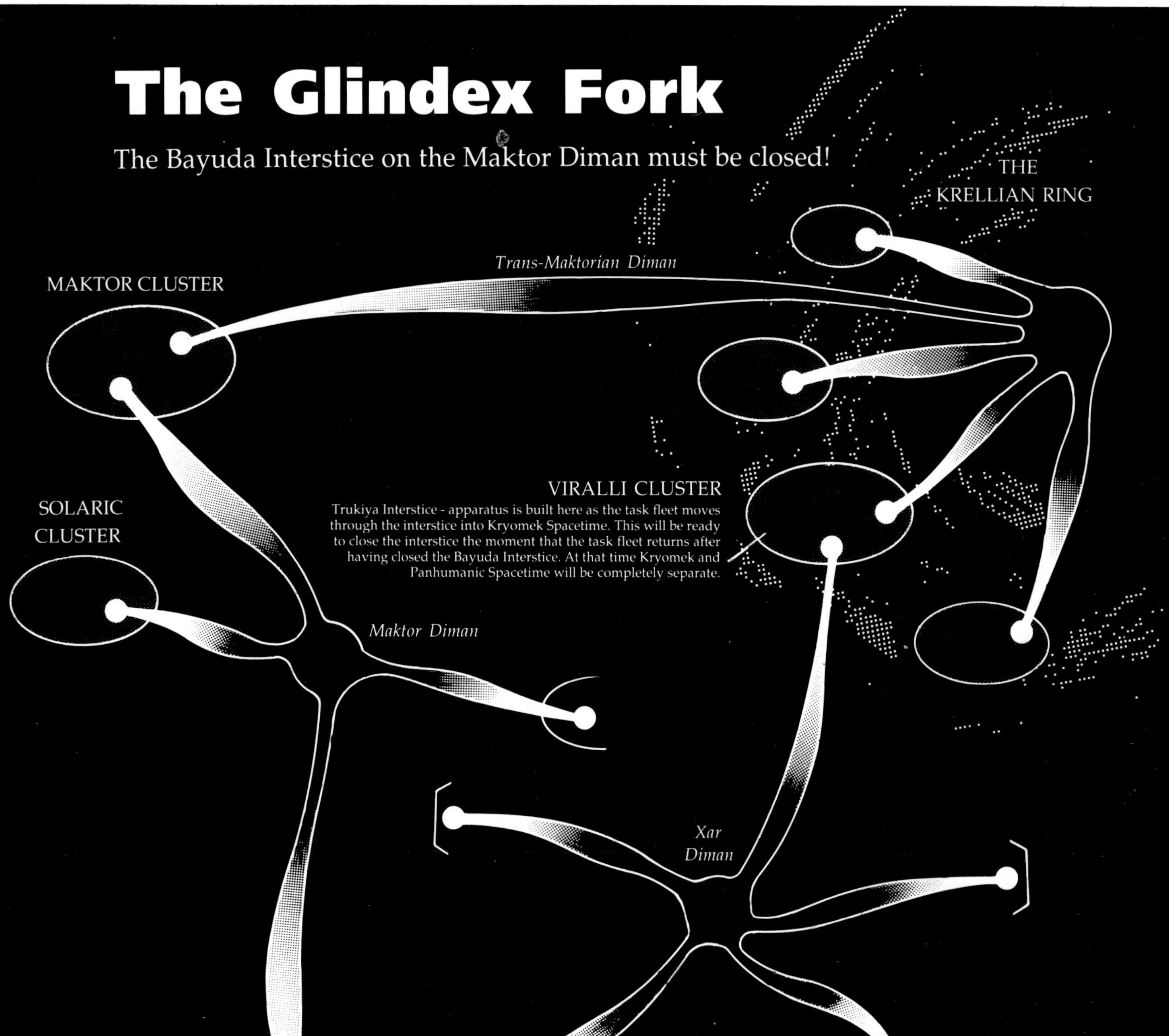

Xar Exclusion Zone is a specially reinforced part of the Exclusion Perimeter which stops the Kryomek gaining access through the Xar Interstice into Panhumanic Spacetime.

CHAPTER

8

Cyclo 'Three-Eighteen'

Cyclo Squad Three Eighteen achieved a momentary, universal fame when they were chosen by a reporter for "Our Times"as a focus for an exposé of the entire Glindex Fork Campaign.

Extract from "The War - Eye-Witness Accounts" ALIS C799.475

580
011
428

First Published in "Our Times" 17.05.3493 IST

When the war started I thought that it was someone else's problem. The next few years were a boom time. The meta-conomy was growing rapidly. My fortune grew with it. I 'harvested' some of the new wealth directly off the compcores of the megacorps. I suppose that I knew that one day I would be caught again. I was already PCB blue[1] from the last time. A second-time conviction would push my PCB rating into the more serious green band[2] but, I had been in their prisons once before and knew the scene - I had more than enough tricreds[3] to make my stay there more than comfortable. I would do my time quietly and after I got out I would leave Irallia - take a ship to some distant world in the Krellian Ring - buy myself a nice spread and retire there to lord it over the natives for the rest of my days. That at least was the plan.

Then they changed the law. The Quorumate announced that the penal code was outdated and needed reform - of course what they really meant was that they needed more cannon-fodder. By that time the War was really hotting up. Three years before, the Hivestone had appeared in Maktor and put the frighteners on the Quorumate. We were not really allowed to know what had happened but rumours spread about the carnage. Then some crazy egg-head at Nexus Central came up with the "Glindex Fork", or some such claptrap. I laughed myself stupid for days until it became obvious that they really meant it. Our boys in laminates were gathered up from all over the place and popped down a di-man into 'monster land'. I wished them luck and got on with making financial arrangements for my old age.

1 Penal Code Band Blue - robbery, embezzlement, fraud etc.

2 Penal Code Band Green - non-fatal violent crimes.

3 Tri-federational Credits - the standard unit of currency throughout Panhumanic Spacetime.

Cyclo "Moonie", CSF 5.7.3.18, was later awarded the Triangulum First Class for his actions in the Battle for Xar. In addition his PCB rating was reduced to blue and he was to be demobbed out of the CSF. These awards and privileges were later rescinded when cyclo Moonie murdered his centurion.

I was caught by a virtual detector[4] that crawled down from a compcore onto my terminal. The bug led the tri-feds[5] straight to me. I went quietly. I was resigned to my fate - as far as I was concerned I had been forcibly retired. I might have been a whole lot less calm if I had known then about the penal reforms.

I was sentenced into the Convict Special Forces in the megatropolis Xirell Nova on 13.04.3492 IST. two months after they changed the laws on mandatory enlistment. Three days later I was transported to the prison moon Gulgatrax.

The reality of Gulgatrax was even worse than that shown in the holopics. I was stripped and left alone in a small cell. Everything was sterile white plastolene. It was only then that I found out how scared a man can get. There was no human contact - just a pair of vidi-scanners tracking me constantly like eyes. I was a rat in a maze.

I screamed and fought like a krelldevil when they came to fetch me for neuro-regulation. They paralysed me with their tancers[6] and strapped me to a surgo-platform. I blacked out. The next thing I knew I was waking with the biggest headache I had ever had - and let me tell you, I've had some of the worst. I felt my head gingerly. My hair had been removed by gausswire[7] and my scalp was still tender. The neuro-regulator was like the stump of a unicorn horn. I was back in my single-piece plastolene shell.

The 'shivers' started in the dark when the cell was lit only by the red glow of my neuro-regulator. It was like fever tremors but much worse. I thought that I was going mad. A man came wearing a plastic mask and said that he was my Trainer. He told me that he had something to make the 'shivers' go away. He made me beg for it. He gave me the tantha and soon the 'shivers' stopped. I threw up. My Trainer told me that I had been poisoned and that only regular doses of tantha[8] would stop the shivers returning. He said that without it I would eventually die in agony.

He trained me like an animal. When I disobeyed he delivered stimuli directly to my pain centres and when I was 'good' he stimulated my pleasure centres. The regulators were both demon and angel - though even the angel had a dark face. Sometimes the regulators didn't work. I saw another cyclo become so addicted to the Pleasure that they had him destroyed.

My body became lean. My hands, soft from the smooth panels of the compcore terminals, became calloused. I learnt to fight with weapons and without. My regulator coaxed miracles of fatigue resistance from my metabolism.

As a passing-out gift the Nexus had our heads surgically tattooed with xaser[9] sensitive barcodes minutely encoded with everything they knew about us. One of our Trainers was wheeled out to tell us that if we were "especially good boys and girls" that in time we might have our PCBs reduced and then it was quite likely that we would be demobbed and allowed to rejoin the panhumanic community. Maybe it was the flat tone of his voice, or perhaps the blank look on his plastolene face, but that speech did not raise my hopes over much.

4 numerical compcore 'organism'.

5 Tri-Federational Internal Security Forces.

6 device for delivering various levels of electro-cardial shock.

7 electromagnetic depilator.

8 erzolar caxumate

9 X-ray Amplification by Stimulated Emission of Radiation (X-ray laser).

I was assigned to a myriad of assault troops on the dreadnought Medusa. We were herded into a transport ship. The smell of fear mixed with stale sweat as we left the prison moon.

The journey was long and tedious. Most of us huddled in our berths. At night they turned the lights down. Our regulators burned like fireflies. During meal times we got a chance to look at each other - everyone was looking around thinking the same thing - 'is he going to be a squadmate?'. There were a few fights - but not many because we all suffered when the Trainers turned up the Pain.

The Medusa was in orbit around Nihiri. She lay between us and the sun, black and monstrous. I caught one last glimpse of beautiful Irallia before the Medusa opened one of her dark mouths and swallowed us.

Her belly was as big as a megatropolis. We cyclos had a quadrant all to ourselves. We never saw the regulars - they never saw us. We liked it that way. The Cyclo-Quad had its own laws - and besides, we wanted neither their pity nor their abuse.

A few days after the Medusa had turned ponderously away from Nihiri we were broken up into squads. There was tension alright. Names were read out - that one last time - after that we would only be known by our unit numbers. When it was my turn I was bolted into the xaser encoder. My scalp tingled as it rewrote my barcode.

From then on I was merely CSF 5.7.3.18 or, within our myriad, 'Three-Eighteen' - I was a labelled part of the Medusa - just another component.

I was locked into a 'socialisation cell' with my five squadmates - I had only expected four - I saw immediately that they had not expected me at all. We were supposed to get to know each other - our lives would depend on it. We were also supposed to 'choose' a squad leader.

They were an unsavoury looking bunch - the kind of scum I'd spent most of my life avoiding. I backed up against the wall. One of them smiled at me. The smile made her seem human. It made me realise that scum or not I needed them. She told me her name was Karah and introduced me to my 'brothers'.

First there was Janor - a surly looking brute. I did not need to be an expert in soma-semantics[10] to tell that he and she were an item. Leaning on him was another brute, Svet. One of his eye sockets was covered by a prosthesopad[11]. The other was well enough to fix me with a baleful stare. Last were 'the twins' - they weren't, but they were actually brothers. One was called Rodix. He seemed to be the quiet one. His brother, Kayfin, was just... strange. He leered at me as if he might want to eat me. I later found out that there had been complications with his regulator - as his brother confided in me tapping his head, "'e's not all there..".

There was little debate when it came to choosing the squad's leader. Janor put himself forward and Svet made his support obvious. Karah was hardly going to protest - and for that matter

10 body language.

11 enhanced artificial optical replacement.

neither was I - Svet's baleful red eye shut my mouth as effectively as the Pain through my regulator would have.

That was that! We were a family. We would live, eat and maybe die together. To the rest of the myriad each of us was indistinguishably Three-Eighteen. Only amongst ourselves did we have personal names.

When the Medusa made the jump through the first diman, I thought that I was dying - or losing what little was left of my mind. The gravitational eddies play more havoc with your synapses than an amber hit. It was over as suddenly as it had come. We made a small trans-dimensional jump and then another diman jump.

It did not take a brain the size of a planet to work out where we were going. Solarica to Maktor - local cluster jump to Bargavus - then the Trans-Maktorian into the Viralli Cluster.

It was all about the Cyclo-Quad, "the Kryomeks.." They tried to keep our minds off it by arming us. It didn't work.

I was dimanwise by the time we took our third and final diman. Afterwards another cyclo told me that she had seen the stuff that they were building to close the Trukiya portal. She said that it had made the Medusa look like a toy. I don't know - I didn't see it myself. I didn't care!

We arrived at Xar on firework night. The Kryomek had breached the Exclusion Perimeter with a Hivestone. They were swarming everywhere. Even in the Cyclo-Quad we could see the lightning flashes from outside. They told us that if the Qatar and the Shiva had not intercepted the kite swarms heading for us we would have come out of the diman to find them already burrowing into our hull.

I huddled together with my squad. We were already a unit. Janor muttered, "holiday's over." If it was meant to be a joke nobody laughed - apart from Kayfin who never actually stopped - not even in his sleep.

He was right though - the holiday was over. We were briefed by our centurions. We had been making for Bayuda to get a gentle introduction into the War. Now we were going to find out about it the hard way.

We had rarely seen our bicenturion. He was probably a hardened 40. It was difficult to tell. Half his face was metal and the other half didn't look happy. One of his arms looked like the flesh had been melted and then poured back into the mould. He had a conference with our squad leaders and then left.

Janor's grim face was even grimmer than usual. "We're going in by twister..," he said as if giving us a sentence of death. "It's tomorrow". Svet grinned. Only Kayfin laughed.

We spent the next few hours being briefed. Janor had a vidislate: the Kryomek had landed a swarm on Xar itself - they were threatening our bases there - we had to exterminate them before they made a hive. Simple really. Our myriad, the 7th, were going down first with the 4th and the 5th. The bicenturion had promised that we would have strider and talos support.

"That's something!" I heard someone mutter.

Janor went for the final briefing with the bicenturion. Svet said nothing - he was keeping his one eye on his battleblade as he sharpened it. The Twins were sleeping. Only Karah seemed to want to talk. We confided our fears to each other. Of all the dangers facing us, we were probably most afraid of the twister descent.

When the time came we were ready. We were given a two-day supply of tantha for our auto-hypos. Our weapons were rubbish - as dangerous to us as to the enemy - but we made them as battle ready as we knew how. There were stacks of ammo.

We left the Cyclo-Quad in irregular lines. Cyclos from the myriads not going looked on sullenly. There were few sounds - just a few scuffles - tempers were short.

We took magnoshunts[12] down to the very deepest levels of the ship - down to the twister cannons that would fire us into the planet atmosphere.

The twister capsules looked innocent enough. We moved forward in squads. As each capsule was filled it slid off into the shadows. We waited our turn. Karah was holding Janor's hand. It was like waiting for a ride at the Grand Carnival in Xirell Nova.

It was soon our turn. Inside, the capsule was cramped. There were six berths - just narrow depressions in the capsule wall. There was some nervous laughter as we fell over each other. An attendant strapped us in. He looked even more nervous than us - but then he was not a cyclo. He snapped the cryogenic hoods closed over our heads and then left after sealing the capsule.

Everyone else closed their eyes. My stomach churned. Kayfin's laughter turned into a cough. The capsule lurched. There was a vibration that lasted for some time. Then there was another lurch and silence.

When we dropped my stomach leapt upwards and my lungs expelled at the same moment. Then there was a terrible screaming sound. As the cryogenics cut in it became more and more remote. My body numbed. The world rolled round and round. I thought I could hear music.

There was a sudden bone wrenching thump and then Janor's voice screaming at us, "Get out! Out!"

I stumbled through the door of the capsule into hell. My head was spinning. My stomach was roilling. The air was filled with smoke. Bullets and shells were screaming constantly over our heads. Just behind us there was a massive roar as another twister hit the ground. I turned and looked up. The sky was full of spiralling capsules.

I was suddenly slapped from behind. Janor grabbed my harness and pulled me after him. "Damn you, Moonie! Get forward!," he hissed. More cyclos were spilling out of the newly landed capsule. Other squads moved forward on our right and left.

12 Electro-grav Transport Tube.

My head was clearing. The twins were running just ahead, bent low. Svet and Janor were on either side of me both of them scanning the grey horizon. Suddenly they froze. I turned to follow their stare. The ground ahead seemed to boil. There was a low rumbling sound. A sound that made my blood curdle - a sound of hissing and of gurgling mucus. The shadows became purple-black spotted with iridescent greens and reds.

I was rooted to the ground with terror as the Kryomek approached like a pack of rabid hunting dogs. I have to admit that I fouled myself. It was only Svet and the striders that saved me.

He slapped me to the ground. The earth shuddered and then a dark shadow passed over us. I raised my head from the mud to see a clawed steel foot as big as a man crash into the earth beside me. The hydraulics in the columned leg hissed and screamed as the foot rose again.

I stumbled to my feet. Svet gave me a quick look of disgust and then ran off to join the rest of the squad nearby. He ran crouched low. Over his curved back I saw the seething mass of Helions foaming towards us. The Goliath was just ahead its ten-tens punching to a regular rhythm. The Helions were exploding as its shells tore through their carapaces but they still kept coming.

As I ran up to the rest of the squad, Janor was getting them into some kind of order. Karah loosed off a couple of grenades but they exploded harmlessly in front of the Helions. There was an uneven line of cyclos stretching to either side.

Somewhere someone started pouring on the juice - the neuroregulators responded to some distant signal. I felt the adrenalin fill me with fire. My arms and legs buzzed. I tried to fight it for it was forcing me forward - forward towards the tide of monsters. I was losing the battle - like clinging to the edge of a cliff as your fingers gradually lose their grip. Svet lifted his head and roared - his one eye seemed as red as his regulator's. He did not want to fight it - he welcomed the battle lust.

Janor urged us forward with a battlecry. We fired our weapons like madmen. I was thrown forward against my will by the fire in my veins.

Still ahead of us the Goliath was strafing the Kryomek mass. Then another strider appeared, a Fenris. It overtook us easily with a few giant strides. It lumbered forward on our right all three of its Kotor annihilators pounding. They were well named. It swung its massive head and sprayed the oncoming tide with shells until it was decimated. We easily totalled the survivors.

We were jumping up and down congratulating ourselves and watching the two striders lumber forward heavily when the Warriors appeared, their curving anvil heads rocking like steam hammers as they ran forward. They were fast - real fast! The striders tried to train their guns on them but they were already between their legs. One of the Kryomek was squashed with a great hiss as the Goliath's foot came down on its head. It was close enough for some of its spraying serum to strike Rodix and burn his arm.

I ignored his screaming. There was a terrible fascination in the carnage and the fire inside filled me with boundless energy. For a moment time stopped. I was watching a holopic and could see myself as a character in it.

The striders were turning around slowly. Their weapons could not target the Warriors. One of them lifted a curving blade and sliced cleanly through one of the Fenris' steel legs. It tumbled forward and twisted into wreckage as it hit the ground. The Goliath started falling back, trying to get the Kryomek that were plaguing it into its sights. The other Warriors kept hacking at the fallen strider until it erupted with a huge violet flash. One of our squads right in the path of the blast was shredded.

When we picked ourselves off the ground we expected the Kryomek to be dead in the wreckage - but first one, then another anvil head appeared out of the flames. We pointed our weapons at them - they came at us - fast! Svet fired his chain-gun at the approaching monsters laughing maniacally. A handful more had appeared from the murk and crashed down upon the cyclo line. I saw the carnage out of the corner of my eye but the fire inside me burned away any terror.

The acrid smell of the Warriors burned my nostrils. Kayfin laughed insanely as he fired streams of ionised needles into the curving anvil head of the Kryomek in front of him. Its screams were like twisting metal. Its blade would have sliced Kayfin in two if Karah had not blown a hole in its chest with a grenade. It fell back, writhing - its tail lashed the ground to dust.

Then I knew a terror so intense that even my regulator was powerless to fight it. Before me rose the great gleaming mass of a Warriors head. It was so close that I could have stretched my hand out to touch it. Its malice was tangible. I was paralysed as it lifted a pronged multi-tubed weapon and pointed it at me. Just the vapours of the bioacid were strong enough to burn my face. My skin itched as it anticipated the stream that would dissolve it.

It did not happen. The monster paused for a split second and then slid away as if it had been called. One moment it was there the next it was gone.

My head would not move. I grated my eyes round in their sockets to follow it. I could not breathe again until it was certainly gone. There was a brassy gleam in the corner of my eye. Five metal men with exposed skeletons of bronze rolled forward like a polished threshing machine. Their synchronicity was perfect. They stepped through the corpses of the fallen cyclos with effortless precision their lifted arms keeping up a constant fire.

My eyes grated round to my right. My squad were wounded or dead. They did not move. Two warriors had their anvil heads wedged in amongst them. The serum leaked out in pools searing the ground.

My eyes were drawn again to the Talos Units. But they stopped before they reached them. There was a shadow there in the murk. A terrible shadow. A lord of monsters. It swayed up higher and higher still on the column of its carapaced tail. I looked back at the

combat between the warriors and the Talos men of bronze, then at the Warmaster. Every motion of the battle was mirrored in its undulations. The Talos Units were the only thing standing between the Kryomek and the rest of my cention. The Warriors were firing their ghastly weapons to great effect. Some of the Talos Units had lost arms, some even their heads. One was trapped powerless in a cocoon of mucous threads. The Kryomek were triumphing. The Warmaster drew itself up to an even greater height. Perhaps it was relishing its triumph.

My hatred for that monster, energised by the rising adrenalin fire, freed me. I fell out of my paralysis and crawled over to my squadmates. Svet was still breathing. If the others were alive I could not tell. The anger grew in me. I prised the chain-gun from Svet's grip and rose to my feet.

I stumbled forward. The regulator burned in my head - the fire spread into my legs. I pounded forward towards the towering horror. The sheen of its carapace sickened me as I came closer. It was holding a massive lance connected by twisting pulsating cords to its head canopy.

I let loose with the chain-gun while it was still swaying back and forth exerting its control over the battlefield. The first shots struck it and flew off as if it were made of lead. It whipped to face me with an ear piercing scream. The great lance swung round like a heavy cannon. I was beyond fear and just kept pouring shells into its hideous bulk. Most of the shells were still glancing off its armour but some were passing through. Hissing fluids gushed from its wounds. I was looking down the length of its lance to the twisted cords that swept up to its carapace. With a sort of fascination I could see them bulging like strings of muscles as it pumped its serum into the weapon. Then I struck lucky. My shells tore through into the soft body beneath and the Warmaster erupted into a fountain of steaming serum.

The lance spouted a huge searing arc of acid but the weight of its massive head as it tumbled to the ground threw the stream to one side. I fell to my knees and passed out.

CHAPTER 9

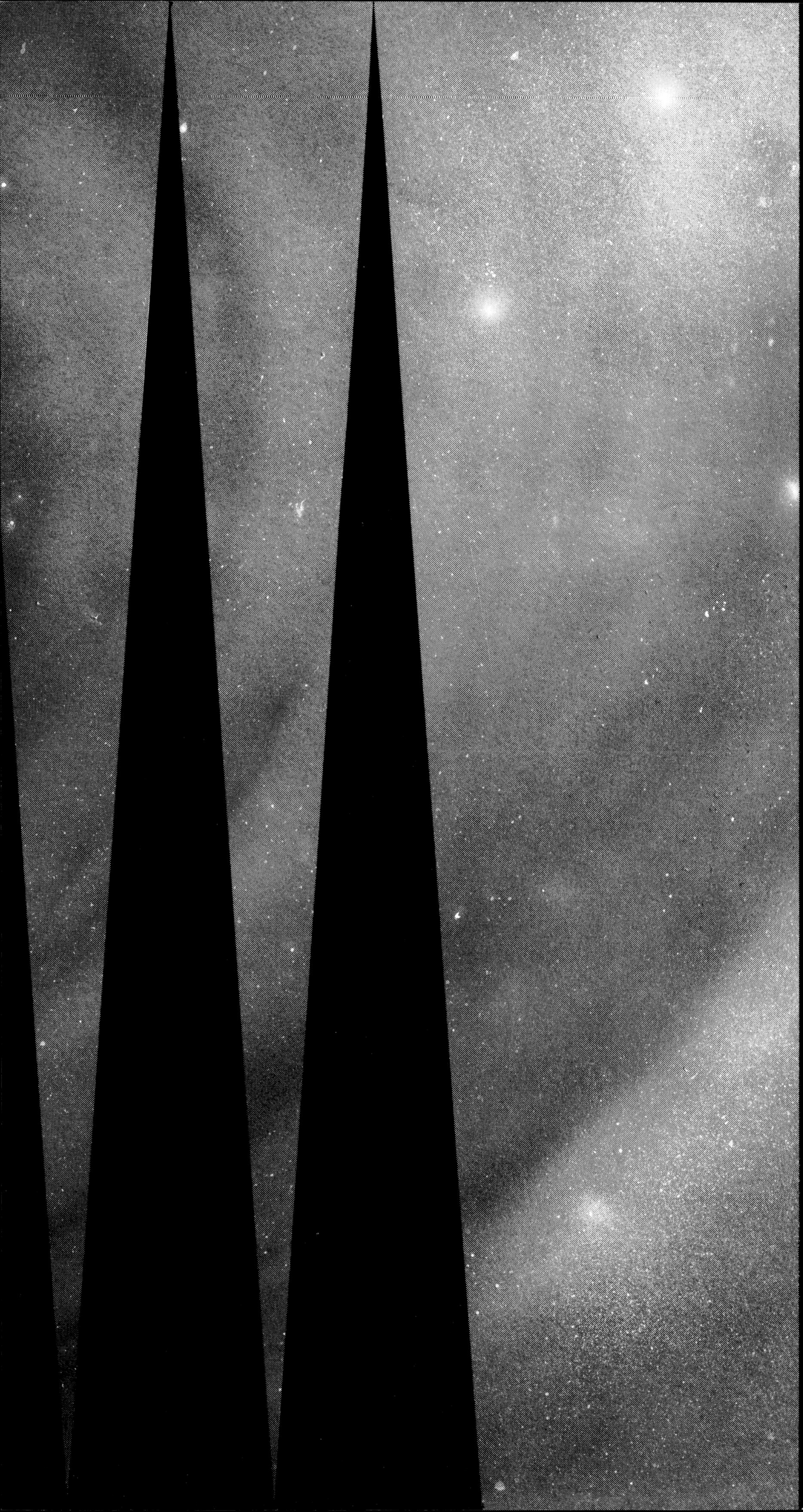

RULES

CONTENTS

The Game

1.1. KRYOMEK

KRYOMEK is a furiously fast, hard fought tabletop skirmish game using the wide range of figures and accessories available from Fantasy Forge.

This book is the first part of a fully integrated Game System that will allow a sophisticated reinactment of the Great Wars between the Nexus forces of Panhumanic Spacetime and the Swarms of the Kryomek Great Hive Hegemony. When completed the KRYOMEK Game System will cover everything from planet-surface skirmish combat to trans-galactic strategic conflict and every level of combat in between.

1.2. The Objective of the Game

In KRYOMEK the objective is to win!

This can be determined in the following ways by:

(i) A Straight Fight - the uncomplicated option in which the winner is the one who inflicts the most casualties.

(ii) Holding the Field - in which the winner ends up in possession of the field of battle.

(iii) Fulfilling an Objective - in which the winner manages to fulfil his objective which can be any number of things - from holding a particular terrain feature to wiping out a particular part of his opponent's forces. (The objective will have to be determined by the players before the game begins. Clearly it is better to choose a mutually exclusive one - where one player can only win at the expense of the other - rather than making it possible for both players to achieve their objectives.)

(iv) A Scenario - in which the winner meets his victory conditions set down in the scenario.

1.3. Key to Diagram Symbols

 Talos Unit

 SWAT

 Marine

 Cyclo

 Warmaster

 Warrior

 Helion

1.4. Game Components

Three A4 sheets are supplied with KRYOMEK containing counters for playing the game. These need to be carefully cut out before the game begins.

Counters for the Nexus player(s)

	Speed Band Counters (Nº 0-7)	**40**
	Move Motivation Counters	**20**
	Fire Motivation Counters	**20**
	Nexus Under Fire Counters	**20**
	Targeting Counter	**2**
	CBU KO Counters	**16**
	Panic Counters	**20**
	Nexus Unit Counters (Nº 1-20)	**20**

Counters for the Kryomek Player(s)

	Control Counters	60
	Targeting Counters	2

Extra Counters

Blank Counters	10

Three A4 acetate sheets.

These contain various types of templates etc. Each of these is labelled on the sheet and has to be cut out carefully for use with the game.

Sheet 1

Area Effect Templates for Bio-Acid Spray, Bio-Acid Jet, Plasmid Cloud-Duster, Spore Launcher and for Direct Placed Deviation

Sheet 2

Area Effect Templates for Grenade Burst, Chain Cannon, Howitzer, Napalm Cannon, Hand Flamer, Heavy Flamer & HAK1010 for Ranged Deviation.

Sheet 3

Turning Key, Burst Templates for Machine / Auto Cannon, Cluster Missiles and a Template for the Corroder Lance.

Card Reference Sheet

For ease of play Reference Strips are provided, one for the Nexus player and the other for the Kryomek player.

Record Sheets

Kryomek Sheet: 4 Warmaster Records.

Nexus Sheet 1: 4 Squad Records.

Nexus Sheet 2: 2 CBU Records, Vehicle Record and Building Module Record.

NOTE: ***Feel free to duplicate any of these sheets to obtain more copies.***

1.5. Extra Components necessary to play KRYOMEK

KRYOMEK is intended to be played using the appropriate figures, models and scenics currently being produced by Fantasy Forge. This range is constantly expanding. Everything described in KRYOMEK is either already in existence or else on the drawing board and soon to be released. Further information can be obtained from local hobby shops.

As new figures, models and scenics are made available further supplements to KRYOMEK will be released. These supplements will provide all the information necessary to incorporate the new releases into the game as well as expanding the game system itself.

In addition to the figures, models, scenics and the various game aids supplied with these rules, KRYOMEK requires at least two D10s (ten sided dice), two D20s (twenty sided dice) and one D6 (standard six sided die). A couple of tape measures or rulers are used to measure distances and pencils are used to fill in record sheets.

The only other requirement is a flat surface (preferably at least 2 x 1.25 m).

Using The Resolution Table

2.1. Determining the Rolling Column

In KRYOMEK many actions and processes are quickly resolved through the use of the RESOLUTION TABLE. In many situations a single D20 is thrown and the Resolution Table is referenced to determine a result.

The Table has 20 columns that are numbered 1 to 20 across the table, and it has 20 rows numbered up the side of the table.

As a general principle, an action (such as an attempt at a ranged shot) will be assigned a BASE COLUMN NUMBER which is a measure of the basic difficulty of the action - the lower the Base Column Number the more difficult the action. The level of difficulty is further refined by applying MODIFIERS (such as range, cover etc) to this Base Column Number. These Modifiers increase or decrease the Base Column Number depending on whether the Modifier is advantageous (positive) or disadvantageous (negative) to give a final ROLLING COLUMN.

2.2. Reading Results from the Resolution Table

Having determined the Rolling Column one D20 is rolled and its score is used to determine the Row Number. The intersection of this Row with the Rolling Column gives the result of the attempted action.

The Resolution Table is divided up into six areas, or ZONES A-F. Results that fall in these Zones have varying results depending on the action being attempted, and are fully explained below. Generally a roll falling in Zone A gives the most successful result and in Zone F gives the worst.

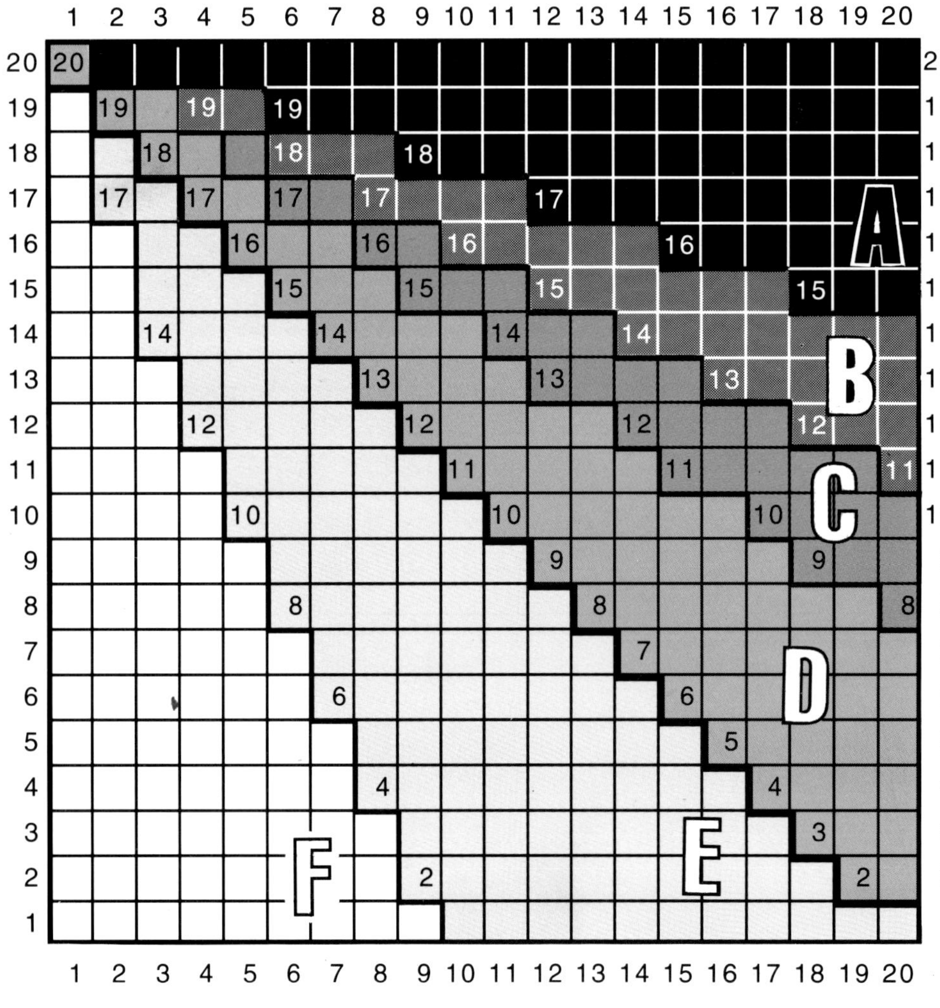

Example: the Base Column Number assigned for an action is 12. There is a positive Modifier +2 and a negative one -3. The final Rolling Column then is 12 + 2 - 3 = 11.

Turn Sequence

KRYOMEK breaks with the traditional Turn Sequence in which either each player takes his turn to move all his units or else some attempt is made at synchronicity with all players moving simultaneously.

KRYOMEK simulates the super-fast command structures of the future (and the swarming chemicoms of the Kryomek) by allowing the player to choose which units he concentrates his attention on. In the KRYOMEK battlefield with its split-second action this means that each side takes turns to activate a Unit. This involves both players all of the time though it does put heavy demands on their tactical decision making.

NOTE: All Resistance Tests are taken and their results applied as and when they are applicable.

3.1. The Turn Sequence

PHASE 1: **MOTIVATION PHASE** - players place Motivation, Control & Speed Band Counters face down beside their Units - thus determining the actions of every Unit. Speed Band Counters from the previous Turn are removed.

PHASE 2: **PANIC & PURSUIT PHASE** - all Units make their Panic & Pursuit Moves.

PHASE 3: **INITIATIVE PHASE** - Both players throw a D10 and the one who rolls the highest gets to choose whether or not to Activate the first Unit.

PHASE 4: **ACTIVATION PHASE** - players make tactical decisions by alternately 'ACTIVATING' each individual Unit one at a time. Squads, Groups & CBUs must complete their movement before firing. Vehicles may fire at any time. In this phase casualties from Ranged Combat are inflicted, Units fall back & Initial Panic Moves are made.

PHASE 5: **CLOSE COMBAT PHASE** - all combats are resolved starting at one end of the table and proceeding Unit by Unit across the table. Casualties from Close Combat are inflicted, Units are pushed back, Initial Panic Moves are made & Resistance Tests to stop Pursuits are taken. [see 13.6]

PHASE 6: **REGROUP & RECOVER PHASE** - Units that were in Panic the previous Turn may take a Test to see if they Recover. Units fragmented by casualties can regroup and become Cohesive.

PHASE 7: **TIDY PHASE** - all Under Fire Counters are turned over. One KO Counter is removed from each CBU.

Initial Setup

4.1. Setup

Before starting the game each player commanding a Nexus force should fill out his Record Sheets. Each Nexus Unit is assigned a unique number from 1 to 20 on its Record Sheet. Players controlling a Kryomek Swarm simply fill out their Warmaster sheets.

Players commanding Nexus forces then place Nexus Unit Counters within the Deployment Area with each Counter corresponding to the similarly numbered Unit on the Record sheets. The player can also deploy half again as many Nexus Unit Counters as dummies to confuse the enemy.

> Example: A Nexus Stratecom has ten Units and can deploy fifteen Nexus Unit Counters - only ten of which actually correspond to his Units.

Kryomek Swarms are deployed freely anywhere within the Deployment Area after the Nexus forces have deployed. If there is more than one such player then they will deploy a Group at a time. (A Group is either 6 Helions, 3 Warriors or a Warmaster.)

All Unconcealed Nexus Units replace the Counters representing them. [see 11.2]

A Player's Deployment Area is defined to be a strip up to 150mm from his edge of the playing area. Nexus Infantry Units can be deployed in buildings.

NOTE: ***Nexus players only have to reveal counters that the opposing player's forces can see. [see 11.1] the rest of the counters remain concealed [see 11.2]***

4.2. Determination of Battlefield Environments

The Great Wars between the Nexus forces and the Kryomek Hegemony have been and are being fought across a bewildering variety of battlefield environments. Fantasy Forge are endeavouring to produce figures and models to match every battlefield type and scenics to simulate every known battlefield environment.

There are several ways to determine the kind of terrain features appearing on the battlefield environment. The environment can be determined:

i) by mutual agreement.

ii) by the particular scenario for the conflict.

iii) by random selection. This could be done by dividing the playing area into areas - for example 250mm squares - and then rolling a D10 for each square:

1-5	no feature
6-8	obstacles - rock outcrops, alien vegetation, pools of liquid methane etc
9-0	main feature approximating in size to the entire square - [see 15]

4.3. Terrain Characteristics

Before the game begins the players must agree the relative heights of any elevated terrain features. This will affect LOS [see 11.1] and allow Units to use the elevation to fire over other Units.

In addition the players must agree on what effects the particular types of terrain is going to have on the Vehicles and other Units taking part. General guide-lines are laid down in the Environment Section. [see 15]

Unit Organisation & Cohesion

5.1. Nexus Troop Types

A Nexus myriad is composed of a complex mix of troop and weapon types each of which has differing tactical characteristics. A myriad can be broken down into three rough categories:

INFANTRY: which comprise the major proportion of the myriad. This category can be further broken down into the ubiquitous Marine or foot soldier (by far the greatest component of Nexus forces) and the Convict Special Forces or Cyclos. Each of these groups has many subdivisions including green recruits and many different types of Elite Units.

VEHICLES: which provide most of the heavy, fast back up for the Infantry. Excluding various stratospheric support craft, the two main types of battlefield vehicles are Striders and a wide variety of Tanks. The former is beginning to supersede the latter.

CBUs: CYBERNETIC BATTLEFIELD UNITS - which are a relatively recent addition to the battlefield. Originally these consisted entirely of cyberized Striders such as the Ksirus Hellcat and its variants. More recently the awesome Talos Units have been introduced and are showing their value on battlefield after battlefield.

5.2. Unit Organisation

All figures are organised into UNITS. The different types of Nexus Unit are called SQUADs, VEHICLEs or CBUs [see 5.1] and a Kryomek Unit is called a GROUP.

Each figure corresponds to a single entity.

Nexus forces consist of human individuals and machines and are structured into a COMMAND hierarchy. Because the individual Nexus soldier has a separate and distinct personality it is necessary to not only lead him but also to MOTIVATE him.

Every Kryomek force is a SWARM. The individual creatures composing this Swarm are of no consequence but merely extensions of their CONTROLLING Warmasters (that are in turn only extensions of the Swarmmaster that is ultimately accountable to its Hivemaster).

5.3. Nexus Human Troops: Experience Rating

All Nexus human troops have an EXPERIENCE RATING which affects their combat ability and reactions.

There are four levels of experience each reflecting a level of training and battle hardening.

GREEN: These are young men just out of basic training with little or no experience of actual combat. "Greenboys" are (naturally) the least reliable of troops and somewhat prone to 'freaking out' at the slightest hint of hurtling lead (never mind seeing a Kryomek in the chitin).

REGULAR: These are the "Grunts" - troops that have survived long enough to know what it's all about - ie. surviving a little longer. They are not much given to heroics.

VETERAN: The 'Old Men' - with the scars of countless battles and a keen instinct for self-preservation. They are best recognised by their idiosyncratic uniforms and their complete contempt for any but the best commanders.

ELITE: The flower of the Nexus military machine organised into SWAT and other elite Units. Warriors picked for their exceptional abilities and then given specialised training.

5.4

5.4. Nexus Units

All Nexus Units consist either of a Squad, a Vehicle or a CBU

A full strength Squad will normally consist of one SQUAD LEADER and four MARINES. Vehicles will have CREWs of varying sizes which are treated as a Squad if they leave the Vehicle.

All human Nexus Units are assumed to be composed of soldiers with the same Experience Rating ie. Green, Regular etc [see 5.3]. However the soldiers in a Unit might be armed differently.

5.5. Nexus Unit Cohesion

To be able to act as a team a Squad must maintain Cohesion. A Squad is COHESIVE if all of its members are within 70mm of the Squad Leader.

5.6. Different Kryomek Castes

A Kryomek Swarm is almost entirely composed of the three different WARRIOR CASTES:

HELION: The rudimentary form of this virulent trimorphic species. The Helion is a ravening war machine: it has no thought other than destruction and it is completely subservient to the commands of its Warmaster.

WARRIOR: A creature taller than a man with a great armoured carapace and armed with a fearsome array of weaponry: everything from single-molecule blades to a range of weapons that project concentrated streams of the creature's own serum.

WARMASTER: Terrifyingly aggressive, cunningly intelligent and very powerful. These creatures use some of the most fearsome weapons in the Kryomek armoury. They have lost their legs and have a greatly enlarged armoured carapace. They exude all the control substances which allow them to control Warriors and Helions.

5.7. Kryomek Groups

Kryomek Groups are always formed from creatures of the same Warrior Caste. These Groups may consist of 6 Helions, 3 Warriors, or 1 Warmaster. [see 5.6]

The number of Groups that are possible in a Swarm is dependent on the combined Control Levels of all the Warmasters in the Swarm. [see 7]

Creatures within a Group may be variously armed and equipped. A Group does not in actuality have a 'leader' (because all Groups are directly controlled by a Warmaster). However each Group will have a nominal 'Group Core' figure which is nominated by the placing of a Control Counter beside it during Phase 4. [see 3.1]

5.8. Kryomek Group Cohesion

A Kryomek Swarm acts as a single COHESIVE entity. This Cohesion is maintained by constant chemical interactions between each of the creatures in the Swarm. The sensitivity of these interactions increases with the size of the creatures so that in a Group a:

HELION: must stay within 25mm of another creature in the Group and 70mm of the Core.

WARRIOR: must stay within 70mm of another creature in the Group and the Core.

5.5 NEXUS SQUAD COHESION

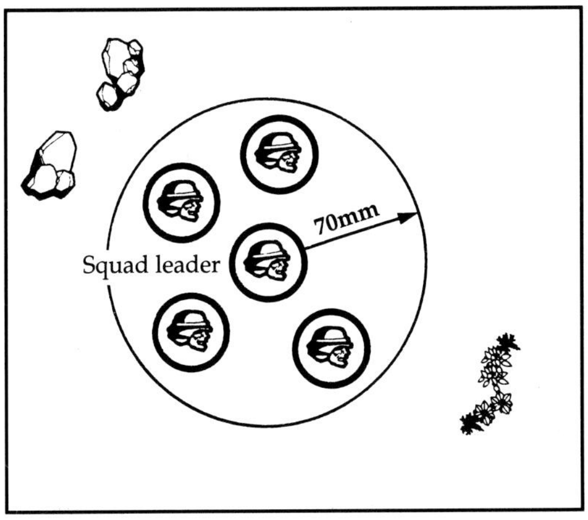

5.8.1 HELION GROUP COHESION

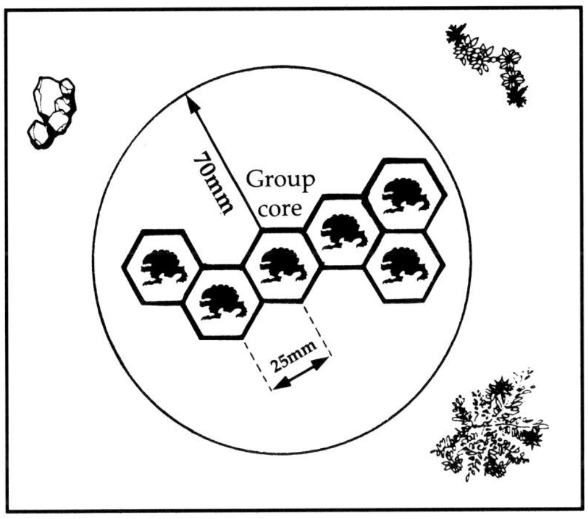

5.8.2 WARRIOR GROUP COHESION

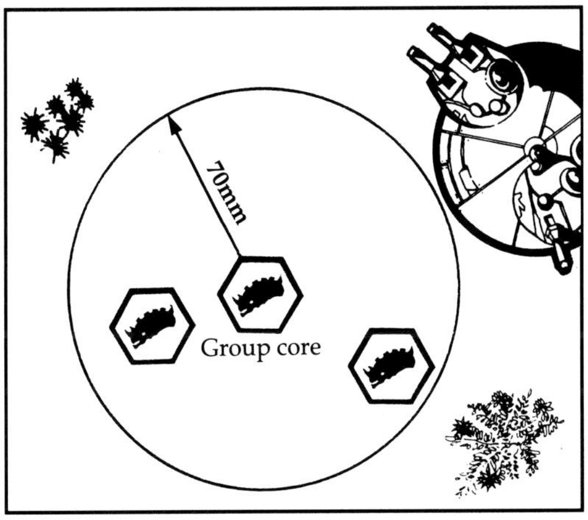

Human Motivation

The MOTIVATION of human Units represents the orders of the Commander (ie. player) as they are passed to each Unit by that Unit's Leader. The successful implementation of the Motivation order depends on many factors such as that Unit's Experience Rating and the battlefield conditions.

It is important to realise that Units are not restricted to only doing what their Motivation orders tell them to do. A Squad can Fire even though it is being motivated to Move - the Motivation only indicates that its Leader is ordering it to Move. Clearly though, in this case, the Squad would not Fire as effectively as if it had been Motivated to Fire.

6.1. Motivation Counters

Motivation for each Unit is determined in Phase 1 at the beginning of each Turn by the placement of an appropriate Motivation Counter beside it. This is true for all Nexus Unit Types except Vehicles and CBUs.

Each Motivation Counter is placed face down next to that Squad's Leader and only revealed when that Squad is about to be Activated. The player may assign a Motivation Counter to each of his Squads.

There are two different types of Motivation Counters:

MOVE: This is necessary for any Squad attempting to either Charge or move when Under Fire. [see 9.4]. Without this Motivation any Squad must subtract 50mm from its maximum Move Distance.

> Example: a Squad without Move Motivation may make a normal move of 100mm but may not make a charge move nor move at all if under fire.

FIRE: This motivation greatly increases the chance of a Squad scoring hits on the enemy - since the Squad Leader insures concentrated and directed fire. Without this Motivation a Squad will fire with a -2 modifier applied when making a Targeting Roll - the Squad is firing at the enemy in an uncoordinated and disorganised way.

6.1 MOTIVATING A NEXUS SQUAD

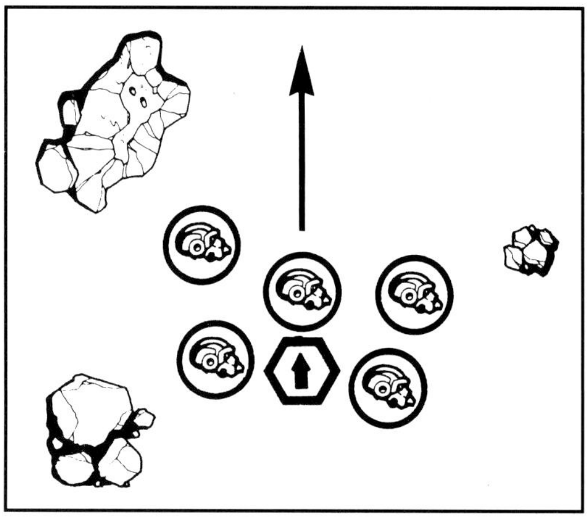

6.2. Vehicle Crew Motivation

Vehicle Crew are always assumed to be Move and Fire Motivated. Instead of allocating Motivation Counters in Phase 1, for a Vehicle the player places a Speed Band Counter face down beside that Vehicle. This will determine in which Speed Band that Vehicle will operate that Turn. [see 10.2]

6.3. Motivation Counters for Concealed Units

Motivation Counters can be placed beside Concealed Units and dummies [see 11.2]. As long as a Concealed Unit does not fire it remains concealed. If the Unit moves out of Concealment or if it fires then it is immediately replaced with the figures that it represents. A dummy counter is discarded once the Unit that it represents is no longer concealed.

Kryomek Control

On the battlefield the Swarm is controlled remotely by the Swarmmaster (in effect the player) that is presumed to be somewhere (off table). The Swarmmaster effects its control through its Warmasters. These in turn exert the minute control over the Swarm Helions and Warriors by means of control substances which they exude and spread across the battlefield.

7.1. Kryomek Control Values

The CONTROL VALUE (CV) is a characteristic of a Warmaster which is a measure of the control that it exerts over the Swarm. The CV is identical to the number of Groups that the Warmaster can Activate and Control within his Radius of Control. [see 7.3].

Each Warmaster may deploy up to 15 Control Counters each Turn. At the beginning of the game (though this might be changed by scenario conditions) each Warmaster has a CV of D6 + 6. This means that it will be able to Activate and Control at most 12 Groups.

A wounded Warmaster will lose some of its CV and with it the Counters that determine its control of the Swarm. [see 14.6]

7.1.2 CONTROLING CORES

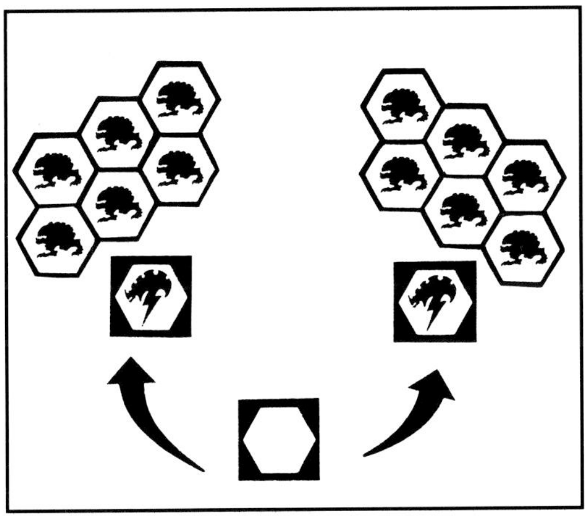

7.1.1 ALLOTING CONTROL COUNTERS

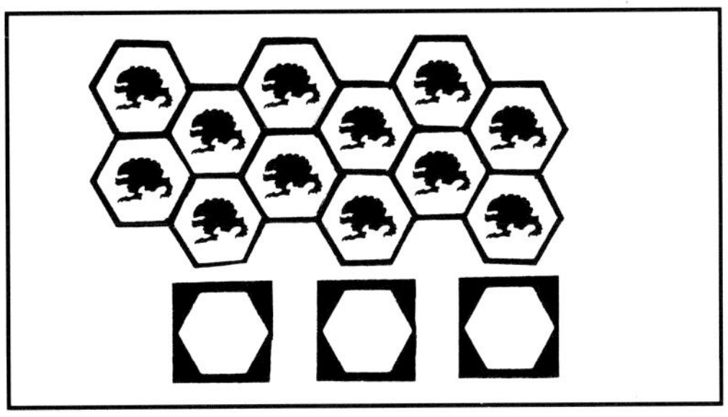

7.2. Control of Warmasters

In Phase 4 a Warmaster is Activated in the same way as any other Unit even though it has no Control Counter of its own.

Additionally a Warmaster may elect to raise itself to its full height thus increasing its Radius of Control [see 7.3]. This is denoted by replacing the Warmaster figure with one in which it is raised to its full height. (If this is not available this can be denoted by placing a blank counter beside the figure.) In this state a Warmaster is more vulnerable to enemy fire.

7.3. A Warmaster's Radius of Control

The range over which a Warmaster can distribute his control substances is limited. This limit is called the CONTROL RADIUS and it varies according to circumstance so that it is:

400mm : if the Warmaster is at its normal height.

600mm: if the Warmaster is erect, raised to its full height - though this does make it more vulnerable to enemy fire. [see 12.25]

The Warmaster can only place Control Counters and form Groups for Kryomek within the limits of its Control Radius at the beginning of the Turn in Phase 1.

7.4. Uncontrolled Kryomek

Kryomek which are outside a Warmaster's Control Radius in Phase 1 are counted as being UNCONTROLLED.

The effect of being Uncontrolled for:

Warriors: is that they go 'shell down' thus presenting a smaller target. They will Defend if attacked but will not Fire.

Helions: is determined by rolling one D10. Then if the roll is:

1-3 the Helions will Move towards the nearest enemy Unit and if within range will Charge.

4-6 the Helions will Move towards nearest Unit and if within range will Charge. (Even if this Unit is Kryomek).

7-8 the Helions will move in a random direction. This is determined using the Ranged Deviation Template.

9-10 the Helions will stay motionless where they are.

Uncontrolled Helions and Warriors will always defend themselves in Close Combat.

Warmasters are always Controlled (by the Swarmmaster off table).

7.3 WARMASTER'S RADIUS OF CONTROL

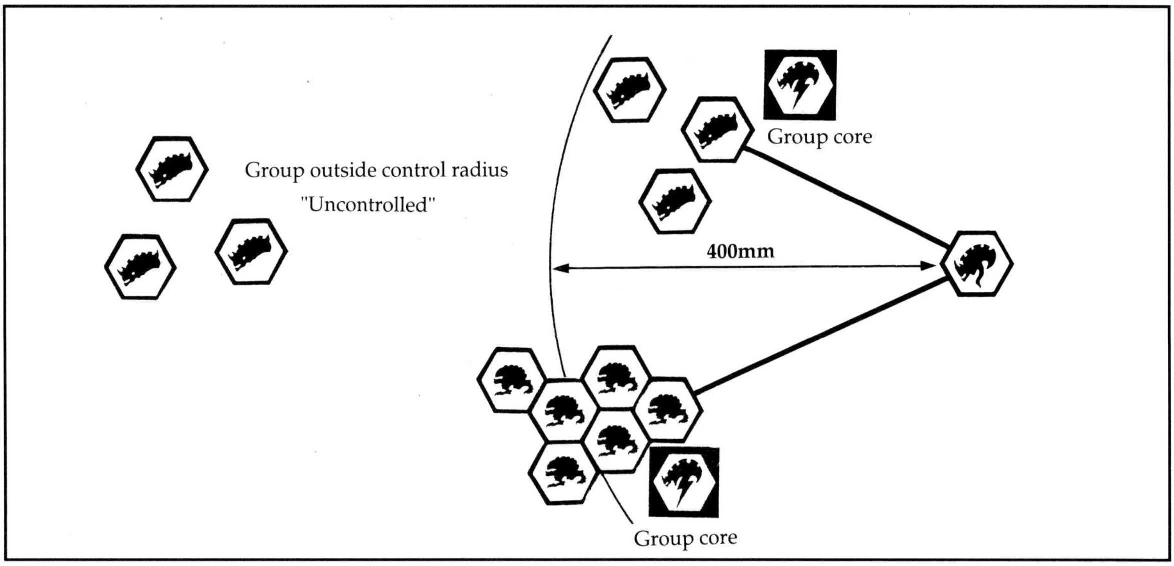

7.5. Miasma

A Warmaster has the capacity to release a miasma cloud which has the effect of masking out much of the olfactory spectrum. The Warmaster tunes the miasma's chemical gradients to still allow clear passage for its control substances. A by-product of this miasma is a rapid decrease in visibility in the area around the Warmaster.

A Warmaster may produce a Level 1 Miasma by relinquishing 2 Control Counters and a Level 2 Miasma by relinquishing 4 Control Counters. These Counters are placed beside the Warmaster during Phase 1.

The Miasma has a shielding effect on all Kryomek within the Warmaster's Radius of Control.

7.6. Placing Control Counters

Each Turn in Phase 1 a Control Counter can be placed beside any figure within the Warmaster's Control Radius. Every such figure will become a potential Core and nucleus of a Group (which will be defined when and if the player turns over the Control Counter .)

In Phase 4 the Warmaster will be able to turn over a number of Control Counters equivalent to its current CV and thus to Activate that number of Groups.

NOTE: *Though a Warmaster will not be able to Activate Groups in excess of its current CV it may choose to Activate as few as it wants.*

Morale

The whole matter of morale and resisting the breakdown of morale is the central notion behind Nexus military training. This is not a weakness that the Kryomek suffer from - as long as a Kryomek is within the Control Radius of a Warmaster it will obey all commands completely. Similarly CBUs, as a conscious emulation of the Kryomek themselves, do not have morale - the emotions of fear and doubt never pass across the logico-neurones of their ACMs.

8.1. The Morale Level

The MORALE LEVEL (ML) of a human Unit represents their willingness at that time to continue fighting. As the ML falls a Unit's Morale begins to waver until finally, when the ML falls to zero, the Unit has reached its breaking point. A Unit that has a ML of zero is assumed to be in Panic and will attempt to flee from the battlefield.

A Unit takes a RESISTANCE TEST under certain precise conditions. [see 8.3 & 8.4]

8.2. Nexus Human Unit Base Morale Level

All Nexus human troops have a BASE MORALE LEVEL (BML) which is related to their Experience Rating as follows:

GREEN:	10
REGULAR:	12
VETERAN:	14
ELITE:	16

In addition, the extra feeling of security experienced by Vehicle Crews because of the extra protection afforded by the Vehicle's armour gives them a bonus of +2 to their BML. This bonus is lost if the Crew abandon their Vehicle.

The BML is modified throughout the game to give the current ML for that Unit. It is this ML which determines the reactions of that Unit to battlefield conditions.

NOTE: The BML is actually the Base Column Number for Morale. [see 2]

8.3. Conditions for taking a Resistance Test: Squads

A Squad must take an immediate Resistance test:

(i) when a Squad loses casualties from Ranged Weapons.

(ii) when a Squad loses a round of combat. [see 13.6 & 13.7]

8.4. Conditions for taking a Resistance Test: Vehicles

A Vehicle must take an immediate Resistance test when it takes damage from a weapon.

8.5. Taking a Resistance Test

When a Nexus Unit takes a RESISTANCE TEST it uses its current ML and then applies any relevant Morale Modifiers [see 8.6] to arrive at a value. This final value gives the number of the Rolling Column in the Resolution Table which is to be used for the Test.

The actual Resistance Test is taken by rolling a D20 and indexing the Resolution Table to obtain the result.

8.6. Morale Modifiers

MORALE MODIFIERS relate to a variety of battlefield conditions and are used to change a Unit's current ML so that the Unit will produce a response appropriate to its situation.

Some of these Modifiers are permanent [see 8.8 & 8.9] and will change a Unit's ML for the rest of the game. Others are temporary [see 8.7] and only change a Unit's ML for the purposes of the current Test.

8.7. Squad Resistance Test Modifiers (temporary)

-1 for each Panicking friendly Unit within Short Range.

-2 if the Unit was Pushed Back during the previous Combat Round.

+1 if the Unit Pushed Back an opponent in the previous Combat Round round.

+2 if the Unit managed to successfully defend a prepared position or linear obstacle.

8.8. Squad Morale Level Modifiers (permanent)

-2 each time a fifth of the Squad's original strength is killed.

-2 if the Squad goes into Panic.

-2 if the Squad is a Crew that has abandoned a Vehicle

8.9. Vehicle Morale Level Modifiers (permanent)

-1 if a Vehicle has lost its Secondary Weapon

-2 if a Vehicle has lost its Mobility

-2 if a Vehicle has lost its Primary Weapon

8.10. The Effects of a Resistance Test: Squads

ZONE A-D: **PASS**: the Unit will hold ground or continue as normal

ZONE E: **FAIL**: the Unit is Pushed Back 50mm if in Close Combat otherwise, if there is cover within 50mm, the Unit must attempt to move into it otherwise it must fall back 50mm.

ZONE F: **PANIC**: the Unit must make an initial Panic Move of 100mm and will suffer a -2 modifier to its ML [see 8.8]. Place a Panic Counter beside the Unit.

8.11. The Effects of a Resistance Test: Vehicles

ZONE A-D: **PASS**: the Vehicle will continue as normal.

ZONE E: **FAIL**: the Vehicle will suffer a -2 modifier to any Targeting Roll for the rest of the current Turn.

ZONE F: **PANIC**: the Vehicle will not be able to Fire until it has recovered and will suffer a permanent -2 modifier to its ML. [see 8.9] Place a Panic Counter beside the Vehicle.

8.12. Recovering from Panic: Squad

A Squad will carry out a Resistance Test.

ZONE A-D: **PASS**: the Unit will recover from Panic remove Panic Counter

ZONE E & F **FAIL**: the Unit remains in Panic.

8.13. Recovering from Panic: Vehicles

A Vehicle will recover from the effects of a Resistance Test automatically next Turn unless it sustains more damage.

Movement: Squads Groups & CBUs

9.1. Types of Movement

9.1 MOVEMENT is measured from the Leader of a Squad, a (nominated) Group Core or a CBU - all the other members of the Unit move forward so that the Unit maintains Cohesion [see 5.5 & 5.8]

There are two types of MOVEMENT:

NORMAL: which is used if the Unit is not Under Fire.

CHARGE: which is used when a Unit attempts to engage another in Close Combat.

9.1.1 NEXUS SQUAD MOVING

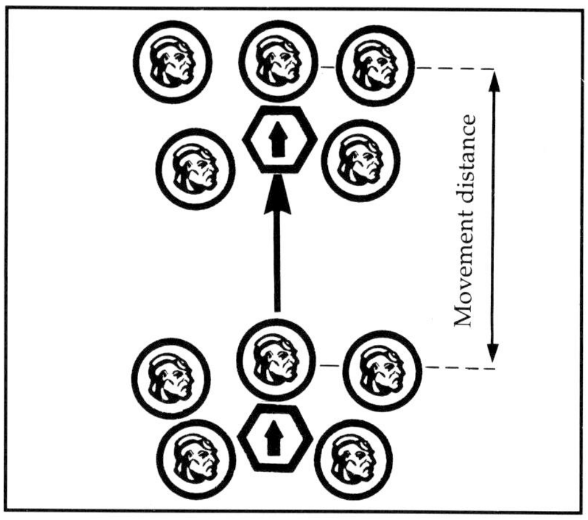

9.1.2 HELIONS MOVING

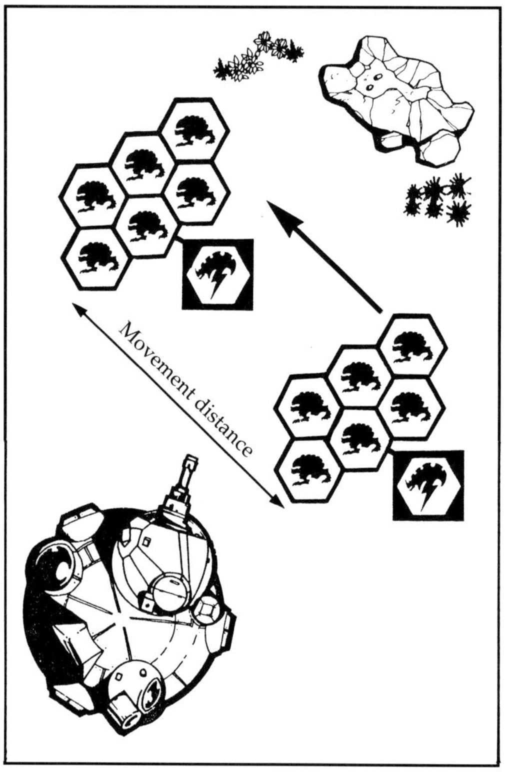

9.2. Movement

The MOVEMENT RATE of a particular Squad or Group is dependent on the type of Movement and is given in millimetres (mm):

	Normal	Impetus	Charge
HUMAN:	150	*D10 x 10+100*	200
TALOS:	150	*D10 x 10+100*	200
HELCAT:	100	*D10 x 10+50*	150
KRYOMEK:	200	*D10 x 10+150*	250

9.3. Movement Motivation for CBUs

A CBU is always considered to have Movement Motivation. However in Phase 4 when a CBU is Activated a spare Motivation Counter is placed beside it to show that it has been Activated.

9.4. Movement Restrictions for Squads

For Squads there are some restrictions to movement:

NORMAL: if a Squad is not Motivated to Move then deduct 50mm from the Movement Rate.

CHARGE: this is only possible if the Squad is Motivated to Move. [see 6.1]

UNDER FIRE: if the Squad is under fire from an enemy Unit then it can only Move if it is Motivated to Move.

9.5. Charging & Charge Impetus

A Charge is made when a Unit is attempting to engage the enemy in Close Combat. The Charge Impetus Move is to determine how 'fast' the Charge 'goes in'. If the Charge Impetus Move would bring the Charging Unit into contact then its target will have no time to react. Clearly this means that a Charge is more likely to be successful the nearer that the Charging Unit is to its target when it initiates its Charge.

If the Unit Leader succeeds in making contact with the enemy Unit then all the other figures in that Unit are also brought into contact.

Any Unit that has Fire Motivation, that has not yet fired and which is not contacted by an enemy Unit in that Unit's Charge Impetus Move may take a Resistance Test. If the result of this is not Panic then that Unit may fire on the enemy Unit before it comes into contact.

NOTE: Any movement that results in a Unit coming into contact with another is considered a Charge Move.

9.6. Movement & Firing: Squads & Groups

Every Squad and Group that is attempting to Move and Fire in the same Turn must complete all Movement before Firing. Charging Units cannot Fire at all.

9.5.1 HELIONS CHARGING MARINES

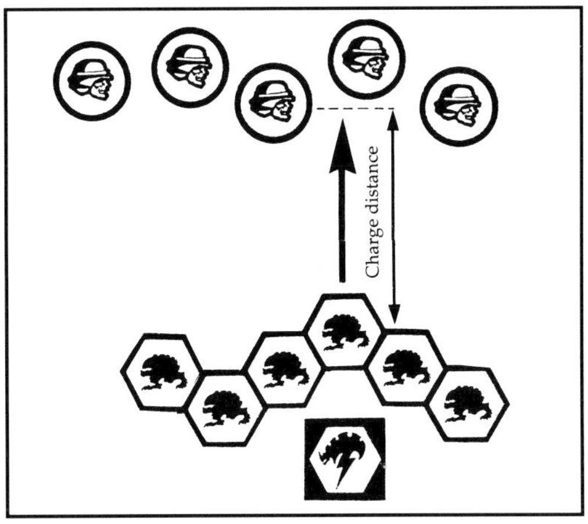

9.5.2 SWATS CHARGING WARRIORS

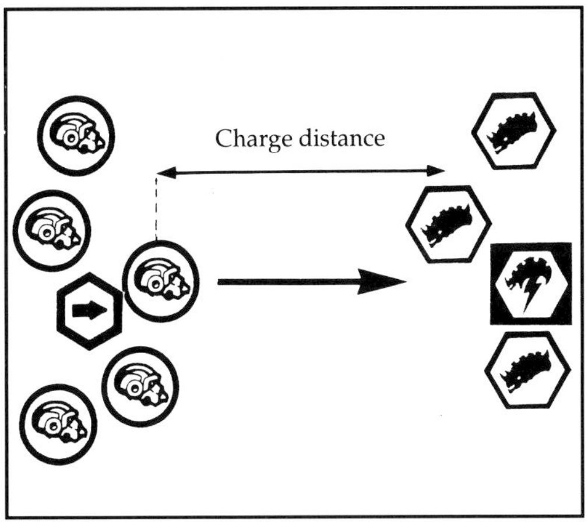

9.7. Units moving through each other

A Unit can Move through another as long as it is completely free of it after it has completed its Move. A Unit is completely free of another if none of its figures are closer to any of the other's than 20mm.

Vehicle Movement

Vehicle Movement is determined by a simple yet comprehensive system which accurately reproduces the effects of acceleration, deceleration and simulates turning by using an acetate Turning Key Template.

10.1. Vehicle Movement Characteristics

A Vehicle has five different MOVEMENT CHARACTERISTICS which describe its mobility. These Characteristics are the Vehicle's:

10.1

Locomotion: of which there are four types:

- **WHEELED**
- **TRACKED**
- **HOVER**
- **STRIDER**

Handling: of which there are five classes which determine how many turns it can make at any given Speed Band:

1 Cumbersome
2 Clumsy
3 Average
4 Manoeuvrable
5 Agile

Top Speed: which is the maximum speed (in mm/Turn) that the Vehicle is capable of attaining in combat conditions.

Acceleration: which is the maximum number of Speed Bands that the Vehicle can increase its speed by in any one Turn.

Deceleration: which is the maximum number of Speed Bands that the Vehicle can decrease its speed by in any one Turn.

It must reduce is speed to the maximum speed in the Speed Band it decelerates to.

10.2. Speed Band Counters

Unlike other Units Vehicles do not use Motivation Counters in Phase 1. Instead a SPEED BAND COUNTER is placed face down beside each Vehicle [see 6.2] and turned over when that Vehicle is Activated. The Counter indicates the range of speeds in which the Vehicle may operate that Turn.

The Counters are numbered from 0 to 7 to correspond to the eight possible SPEED BANDS [see 10.3]. In Phase 1 each new Counter is placed beside the previous one. The new Speed Band must be within the Acceleration / Deceleration limits of the previous one.

> Example: a Vehicle has an Acceleration of 2 and a Deceleration of 2 and travelled at Speed Band 4 in the previous Turn. The new Speed Band Counter cannot be more than 2 higher (ie. 6) or 2 lower (ie 2) relative to the previous Speed Band.

Once the Counter has been placed for a Turn the vehicle MUST move a distance which lies within the limits of the chosen Speed Band.

> Example: if a Speed Band 3 Counter is placed the Vehicle has to be moved not less than 330mm nor more than 480mm that Turn [see 10.3]

10.3. Speeds and Speed Bands

Each SPEED BAND represents a possible range of up to 160mm of actual movement on the table. These Bands are defined as follows:

0	0mm - stopped
1	10-160mm
2	170-320mm
3	330-480mm
4	490-640mm
5	650-800mm
6	810-960mm
7	970-1120mm

> Example: a Vehicle travelling in Speed Band 5 could move any distance between 650mm and 800mm. The actual distance moved within these limits is decided by the player when he moves the Vehicle.

10.4. Reversing & Turning on the Spot

All Vehicles may reverse at Speed Band 1. This is indicated by putting the dust cloud on the Speed Band Counter at the front rather than the back of the Vehicle.

Vehicles at Speed Band 0 are stationary and cannot move at all that Turn except for Vehicles that:

HOVER: which may turn on the spot up to 90° in either direction

WALK: which may turn on the spot up to 45° in either direction

are **TRACKED:** which may turn on the spot up to 45° in either direction

NOTE: ***Wheeled Vehicles may not turn on the spot at all - they must be moving to be able to turn.***

10.5. Vehicle Handling Classes

The HANDLING CLASS (HC) of a Vehicle determines the maximum number of turns it can make during one game Turn. Thus a Vehicle of the following Handling Classes will have the associated numbers and types of turn:

HC 1: one 45° turn.

HC 2: two 45° turns.

HC 3: three 45° turns.

HC 4: four 45° turns, or two 45° & one 90° turn

HC 5: four 45° turns or two 90° turns

The angles given above (ie. 45° or 90°) are only the maximum limit for the turn and any turn angle up to these may be made. The maximum number of turns allowed must never be exceeded.

NOTE: ***90° turns are only possible to Vehicles moving at Speed Band 1.***

> Example: if a Vehicle with HC 2 were to have already made two turns even though they were small ones (10° and 25° for example) this does not entitle it to make another one - however small it might be.

10.6. The Turning Key

10.6 THE TURNING KEY

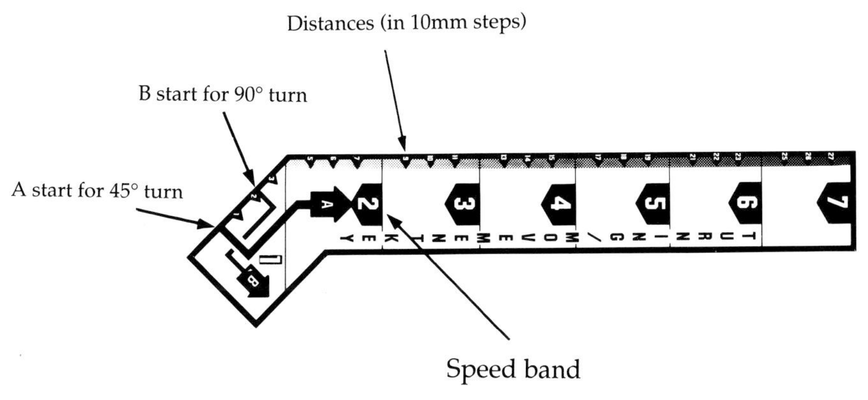

10.7. *Using the Turning Key to make 45° turns.*

(i) Place the Turning Key so that its point A is lined up with the rear of the Vehicle (on the side to which the Vehicle is turning) - see diagram.

10.7.1 VEHICLE TURNING 45° (1)

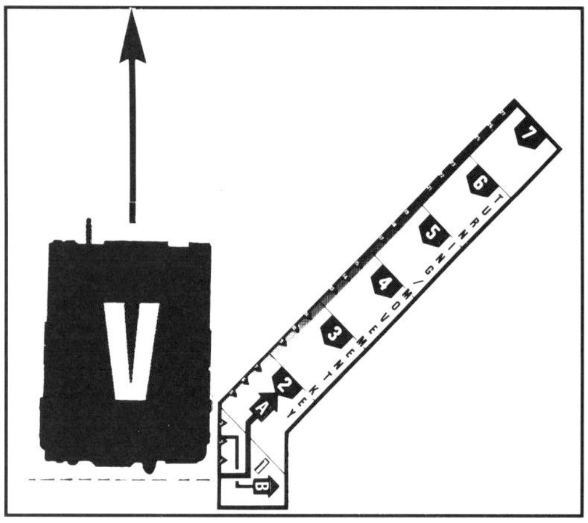

(ii) Move the Vehicle alongside the Turning Key until the rear of the Vehicle is lined up with the number on the Turning Key that corresponds with the Speed Band that the Vehicle is travelling at- see diagram.

The Vehicle will have performed a 45° turn. The distance travelled while making the turn is shown in smaller digits along the edge of the Turning Key. This distance counts as part of the Vehicle's total Movement that Turn.

10.7.2 VEHICLE TURNING 45° (2)

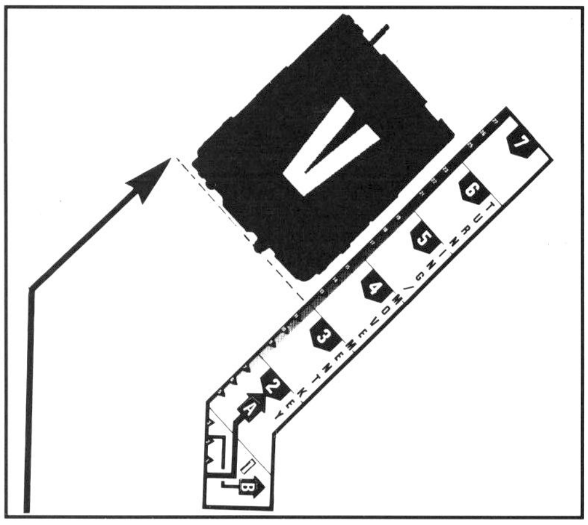

10.8. *Using the Turning Key to make 90° turns.*

(i) Place the Turning Key so that its point B is lined up with the rear of the Vehicle (on the side to which the Vehicle is turning) - see diagram.

10.8.1 STRIDER TURNING 90° (1)

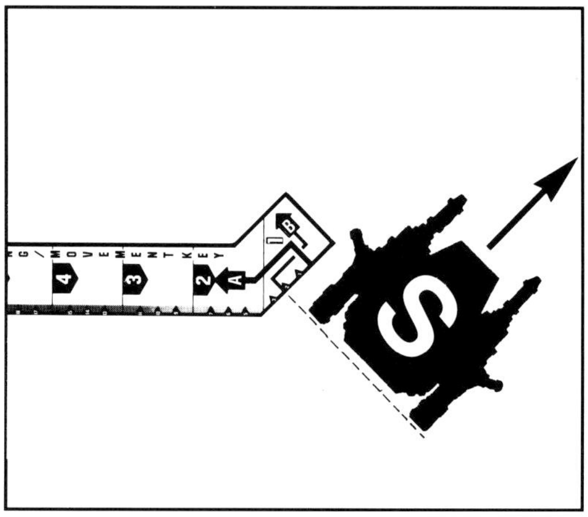

(ii) Move the Vehicle around the square end of the Turning Key.

The Vehicle will have performed a 90° turn. The distance travelled while making the turn is 40mm. This distance counts as part of the Vehicle's total Movement that Turn.

10.8.2 STRIDER TURNING 90° (2)

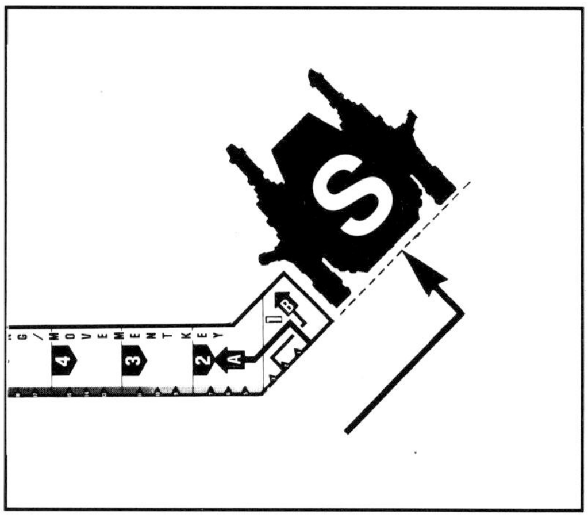

10.9. Vehicles: Moving & Firing

Vehicles may fire their weapons at any time during Phase 4 even if they are Moving.

Each weapon on a Vehicle may only fire once per Turn. If the Vehicle is armed with multiple weapons systems that are mounted independently it may fire each of them at different targets during the Turn. Weapons that are Multiply Mounted such as for example twin guns on the same mounting must fire together at the same target. [see 11.13]

If a Vehicle has to take a Resistance Test due to Bad Terrain at any point in its movement and failed the Test, it may not fire any more weapons in that move. [see 15.5]

10.10. Troops Entering or Leaving a Vehicle

One Squad can enter or leave a Vehicle by each of its doors each Turn. This process is subject to the following restrictions:

ENTERING: the Squad wishing to enter must be within half a move's distance of the Vehicle and be Move Motivated.

LEAVING: the Squad wishing to leave the Vehicle must be Move Motivated. It can move up to half its Normal Move distance.

A Squad attempting to enter or leave a Vehicle that has not been Activated must make a Safety Check. This Safety Check is made by momentarily revealing the Vehicle's Speed Band Counter. A Squad can safely enter and leave any Vehicle travelling at Speed Band 1. It is impossible for a Squad to enter any Vehicle travelling faster than this. Leaving a Vehicle becomes increasingly hazardous with increasing speeds.

Make a Damage Roll [see 14.1] using the following Impact Modifiers that correspond to the appropriate Speed Band. If the Speed Band is:

2 Modifier is -3

3 Modifier is 0

4 Modifier is +3

5 Modifier is +6

6 Modifier is +9

7 Modifier is +10

10.11. Movement of Squads through Buildings

Squads may be moved into Modules [see 15] subject to the capacity of the Module. [see Hardware]. A Squad that is inside a Module is considered to be Concealed [see 11.2]. The figures making up the Squad are removed and a Nexus Unit Counter is placed on the Module to indicate that they are inside.

At the beginning of the game these Counters may be deployed in this way to indicate that the Units are to start within them. [see 4.1].

A Squad can be moved through a Complex of Modules at half its normal Move. A Squad takes half of its Movement Phase to enter or exit a Module via its airlock.

At all times dummy Nexus Unit Counters can be deployed to confuse the enemy.

Combat: Basic Concepts

11.1. Drawing Lines of Sight

A LINE OF SIGHT (LOS) is any direct line that can be drawn between two Units. For the LOS to be CLEAR it must not pass through any body such as a Unit, Terrain feature or any other Obstacle [see 15] and if it passes through a gap between two such bodies that gap must be at least 50mm wide. An LOS that is not Clear is OBSTRUCTED.

11.1.1 LINE OF SIGHT (1)

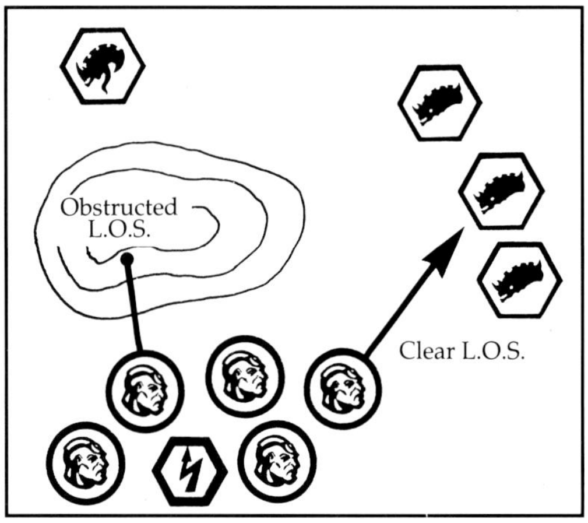

11.1.2 LINE OF SIGHT (2)

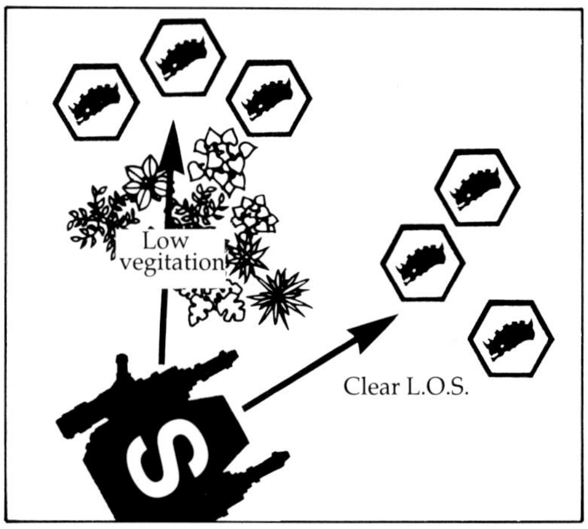

11.1.3 LINE OF SIGHT (3)

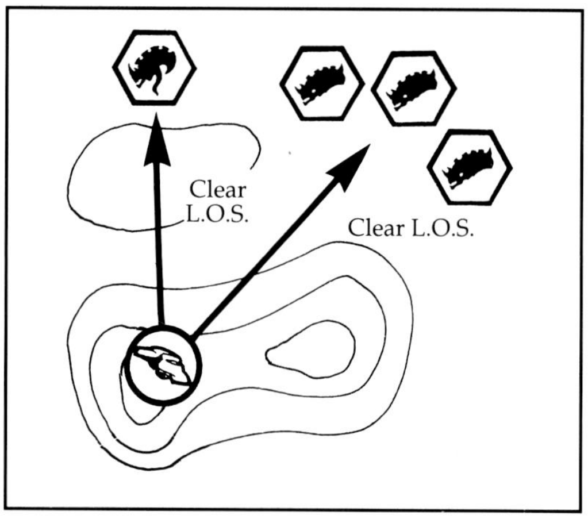

11.2. Concealed Units

A Unit is considered CONCEALED if it is within a Module or concealed by some other Terrain Feature and remains Concealed until it either moves out of Concealment or else Fires.

11.3. Weapon Types

There are four basic types of weapon:

i) Direct Fire Weapons: these can be used both in Ranged and Close Combat. (eg. a pulse rifle).

ii) Close Combat Weapons: these can only be used in Close Combat. (eg. Single-Molecule Blades, Xenoid Stick etc.)

iii) Ranged Area Effect Weapons: these can only be used in Ranged Combat. (eg. a grenade launcher).

iv) Directly Placed Area Effect Weapons: these can be used both in Ranged and Close combat but in the latter they sometimes change into Direct Fire Weapons. (eg. corroder lance).

[see Hardware]

11.4. Armour Categories

There are two basic ARMOUR CATEGORIES:

SOFT: Nexus Power Armour, Kryomek carapaces etc.

HARD: Armoured Vehicles, reinforced buildings and other battlefield architecture.

11.5. Armour Classes

An ARMOUR CLASS is a rating of how strong a type of armour is. There are two scales one each for the two Armour Categories: Soft and Hard.

NOTE: ***The Armour Class is actually the Base Column Number for Damage Roll. [see 2]***

11.6. Kryomek Armour Classes

The chitinous carapaces of the Kryomek, strengthened with a wide variety of exotic biopolymerized resins, perform as an extremely effective form of Soft Armour. The Armour Classes for these are as follows:

WARMASTER: 2

WARRIOR: 4

HELION: 8

11.7. Human Armour Class

The skin of an unarmoured human provides little resistance to any commonly used weaponry. The Armour Class for a human is:

HUMAN: 10

11.8. CBU Armour Classes

CBU armours vary with the model of the Unit. [see Hardware]

11.9. Weapons Modifiers

A Weapons effectiveness in Combat is expressed by five separate factors:

ACCURACY: the Accuracy Modifier is applied when making a Targeting or Strike Roll.

RANK: this is the number of Hits that the weapon is capable of inflicting on a successful Targeting or Strike Roll.

IMPACT: the Impact Modifier is applied to change the Rolling Column when making a Damage Roll.

HAP: Hard Armour Piercing capability

SAP: Soft Armour Piercing capability

[see Hardware]

11.10. Primary and Secondary Functions

Vehicles and Modules may have PRIMARY and SECONDARY FUNCTIONS (or WEAPONS).

> Example: A hover tank with HAK 1010 Cannon as Primary Function (or Weapon) and HAK B17 fm machine gun - as a Secondary Function (or Weapon).
>
> Example: A command dome with a sensor tower being its Primary Function and with a sentinel tower with twin mounted light machine guns as a Secondary Function.

11.11. Additional Weapons

Kryomek and CBUs may use ADDITIONAL WEAPONS without restriction.

> Example: A Kryomek Warrior in Close Combat with two single-molecule blades strikes with each weapon independently. This is as if the weapons were being wielded by two separate creatures.

Nexus Humans using more than one weapon must nominate a PRIMARY WEAPON.

Weapons may be either one-handed or two-handed. [see Harware]

The Primary Weapon gains its full bonuses while the other gains a bonus as an ADDITIONAL WEAPON.

If an Additional Weapon is being used add a Modifier of +1 the Targeting or Strike Roll irrespective of the weapons bonuses.

Additional weapons only gain a bonus if they are capable of affecting the Armour Category of the target [i.e. soft/hard] [see 11.4]

11.12. Fixed Mounted Weapons

Any weapon that is FIXED MOUNTED onto a Vehicle or Module has its Arc of Fire restricted to the Swivel Arc of the turret [see Hardware] if it is turret mounted or else to the orientation of the hull if it is hull mounted [see Hardware]

11.13. Multiple Fixed Mounted Weapons

Multiply Fixed Mounted Weapons are said to form a MULTIPLE MOUNTING. A Multiple Mountingsis made up of identical weapon types. A Mounting has certain advantages and are subject to certain restrictions:

(i) a Mounting is considered to be an enhanced single weapon.

(ii) if a Mounting is made up of Direct Fire Weapons then it must target a single Unit.

(iii) if a Mounting is made up of Area Effect Weapons then these must fire into a single Area Effect Template for that type of weapon.

(iv) a Mounting adds a +1 Modifier to a Targeting or Strike Roll for each additional weapon in the Mounting .

(v) a Mounting increases the Impact of its weapons by 1 for each additional weapon in the Mounting.

> Example: The Storm Strider series Fenris with triple fixed mounted Kotor ACG12 Assault Chain Cannons targets a Group of Kryomek Warriors. A Chain Cannon Area Effect Template is placed according to standard practise though a +2 Modifier is applied to the Targeting Roll. When determining the affect on the Kryomek, the Fenris makes a Damage Roll with a + 2 Modifier.

Ranged Combat

12.1. Ranged Combat Ability

RANGED COMBAT ABILITY reflects the proficiency that a Squad or Group has with Ranged Weapons.

Ranged Combat Ability is directly related to Experience Rating for Nexus Human Troops [see 5.3] and to the different Warrior Castes [see 5.6] amongst the Kryomek as follows:

GREEN:	6	**TALOS:**	10
REGULAR:	8	**HELION:**	n/a
VETERAN:	10	**WARRIOR:**	8
ELITE:	11	**WARMASTER:**	9
HELCAT:	8		

12.2. Weapon Range Bands

There are four RANGE BANDS. Some weapons are effective against targets at all Range Bands while others may be restricted. [see Hardware]

The Range Bands are:

CLOSE:	Up to 300mm
MEDIUM:	From 300mm to 600mm
LONG:	From 600mm to 900mm
EXTREME:	From 900mm to 1200mm

There are some specific weapons that are virtually unlimited. [see Hardware]

NOTE: The Ranged Combat Ability is actually the Base Column Number for Ranged Combat. [see 2]

12.3. Measuring Firing Ranges

When a Squad or Group fires at an enemy Unit the range is always measured from the centre of the Leader figure of the firing Unit to the nearest figure of the enemy Unit.

When a Vehicle fires one of its weapons at an enemy Unit the range is always measured from the front of the Vehicle (or else from the end of the weapon barrel) to the nearest figure of the enemy Unit.

This range is placed within the appropriate Range Band. All the weapons of the figures in the firing Unit are assumed to be firing within that Range Band.

> Example: The Squad in the Diagram is firing at Warriors. The range between the Units is 330mm so that the Squad's weapons are being fired in the Medium Range Band - despite the fact that the LEADING figures in each Unit are in fact 300mm apart.

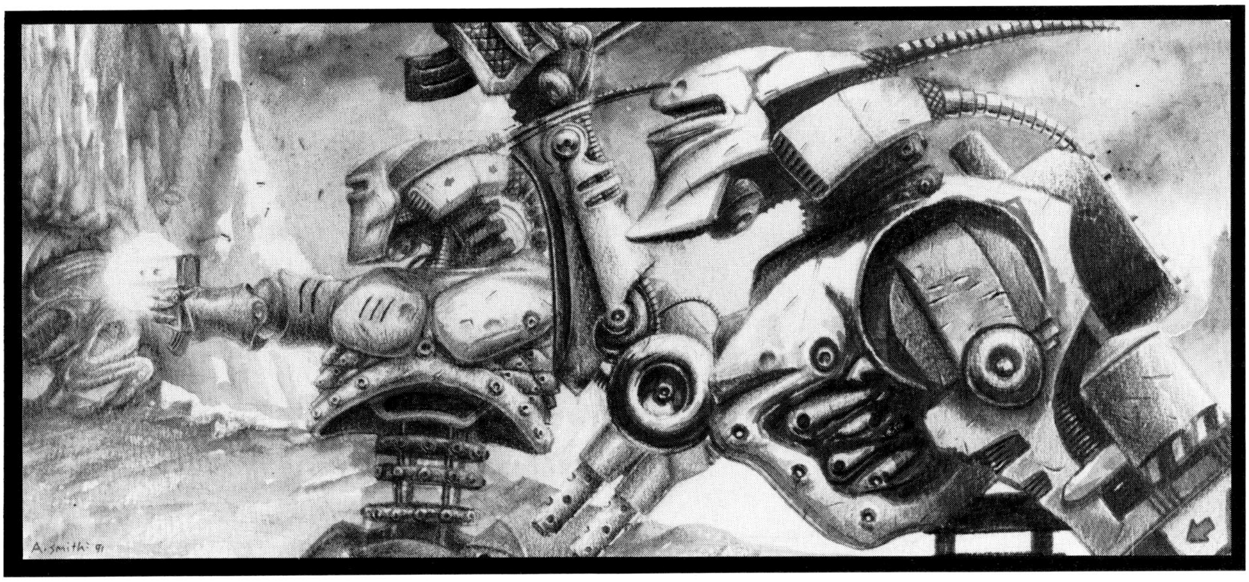

12.3 MEASURING FIRING RANGE

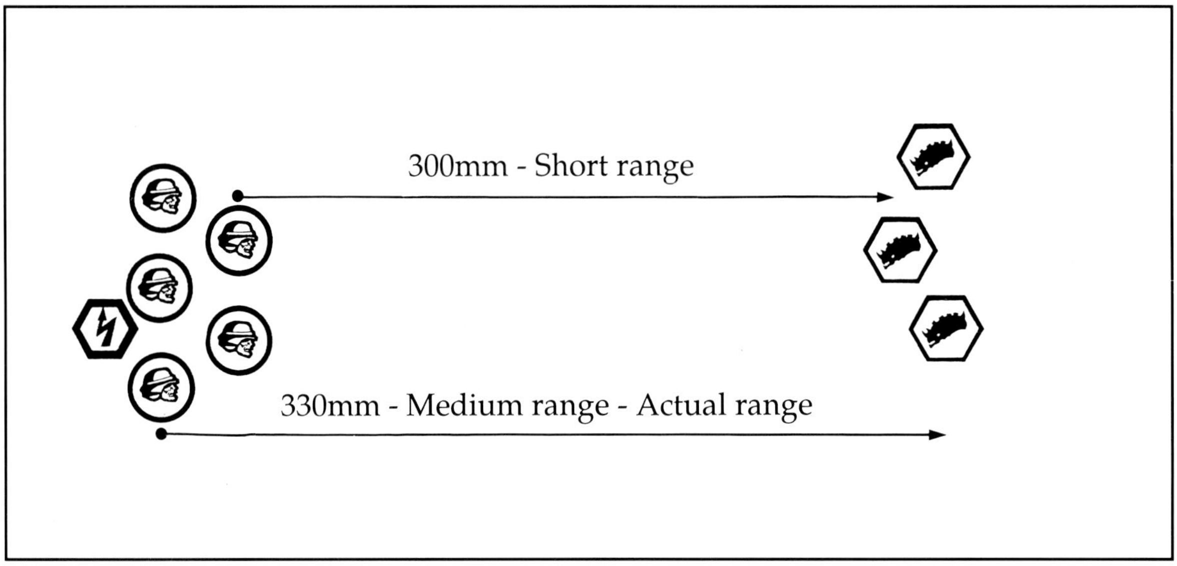

12.4. Firing Arcs

All figures in a Unit face forward in that Unit's direction of movement. The FIRING ARC for all figures in that Unit is 90° to either side of this direction of movement.

12.4 ARCS OF FIRE

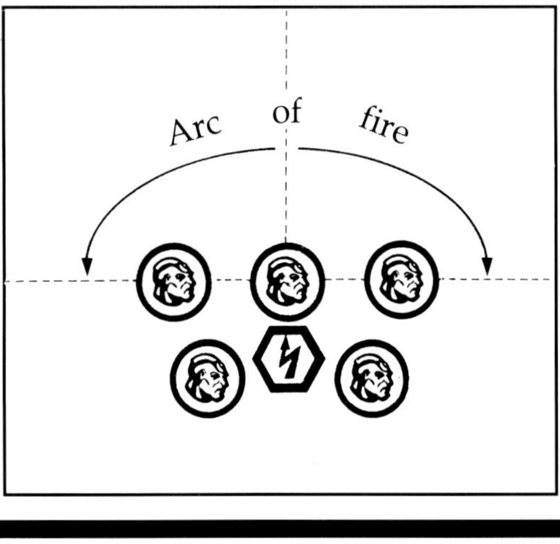

12.5. Line of Fire

A LINE OF FIRE is a straight line drawn between a firer and its target.

12.6. Firing Eligibility

A Unit can fire at any target that is within range of any of its weapons and to which it has a Clear LOS. Any figure in that Unit that can draw a Clear LOS to any figure in the target Unit can fire at it.

12.7. Target Priorities for Nexus Human Units

Battlefield conditions will have a great bearing on a Human Unit's choice of what to fire at - troops are expected to make their own on-the-ground decisions on the threat that different enemy units present to them. They will be tempted to fire at the one they feel is the most dangerous to their personal survival.

To simulate this a Unit may fire freely except if there is a target Unit within Close Range and if there is more than one at the nearest of these.

Vehicles will as a preference target enemy Units that appear to have Hard Armour Piercing capability. [see 11.4] since these will have the greater capacity to harm it.

12.8. Target Priorities for CBUs

Helcats must fire on nearest enemy Units but Talos Units, however, with their series X5 ACMs have complete freedom of target choice.

12.9. Splitting Fire

In general a Unit will only fire at a single target each Turn. However, in certain circumstances a Unit might want to split its fire between two or more targets.

> Example: if a single Squad was under attack by two Kryomek Groups advancing on it, and there were no friendly troops around to give supporting fire, the Leader could decide to split the Squad's fire between the two targets

A Unit's fire may be split subject to the following restrictions:

i) The division of fire (i.e. which figure is firing at which target) must be decided and announced before any dice are rolled for hits.

ii) Only one of the attacks (i.e. all the figures firing against one target) counts as being Motivated [see 6.1]. The other attacks suffer the penalty for not being Fire Motivated.

> Example: a figure in a Squad has an anti-vehicle rocket launcher. In this case this could be fired against an enemy Vehicle, while the other members of the Squad could fire their weapons at another nearby Unit of Infantry.

12.10. Cover

There are two types of COVER which are analogous to the two Armour Categories [see 11.4]:

SOFT: which makes a Unit more difficult to hit but does not reduce the impact damage ie. trees, wooden fences, foliage etc

HARD: which makes a Unit more difficult to hit and also reduces the impact damage ie. concrete walls, metal wreckage, trenches etc.

12.11. Effects of Cover

All types of Cover cause a -2 modifier to be applied to any Targeting Roll. Hard Cover causes an extra -2 modifier when making a Damage Roll. [see 12.12]

12.12. Rolling Columns: Ranged Combat

Ranged Combat is determined by means of a TARGETING ROLL made on an appropriate Rolling Column.

To determine the Rolling Column [see 2] for a ranged weapon take the Ranged Combat Ability for the figures or model firing and apply the following modifiers:

MOTIVATION:	Unmotivated (Nexus)	-2
FIRER STATUS		
Squad /Group:	Moving	-2
	indirect fire	-3
Vehicle:	each Speed Band	-1
TARGET STATUS:	each Speed Band	-1
	non-erect Warmaster	-1
	"shell down" Warrior	-1
	level 1 Miasma	-1
	level 2 Miasma	-2
	in cover	-2
	each Size increment of 6	+1

12.13 Under Fire

A Squad is classed as being Under Fire if:

(i) any Direct Fire Targeting Rolls have been made against it. [12.15]

(ii) any Area Effect Templates have been placed within 100mm of any of its figures.

A Unit that comes Under Fire has an Under Fire Counter placed face down beside it.

12.14. Indirect Fire

Any INDIRECT FIRE WEAPON can be fired at a target over an intervening friendly Unit as long as the firer is within 100mm of that Unit. The Targeting Roll is however subject to a -3 Modifier.

12.15. Targeting Rolls: Direct Fire

Having determined the Rolling Column the Targeting Roll is made by rolling one D20 to determine the result on the Resolution Table. [see 2].

The actual result does depend a lot on the RANK of the firing weapon:

<u>Rank 1</u>

The result depends in which Zone of the Resolution Table the roll lands:

Zones E & F: a miss

Other Zones: cause 1 Hit.

Rank 2

The result depends in which Zone of the Resolution Table the roll lands:

Zones E & F:	a miss
Zones C & D:	cause 1 Hit
Zones A & B:	cause 2 Hits

Rank 3

The result depends in which Zone of the Resolution Table the roll lands:

Zones E & F:	a miss
Zone D:	causes 1 hit.
Zones B & C:	cause 2 hits.
Zone A:	causes 3 hits.

12.16. Allocating Hits

In all cases in which Infantry Units are targeted with Direct Fire Weapons it is necessary to work out which figures comprising that Unit were hit. The procedure for doing this is as follows:

1. Pick the nearest figure in the Unit in LOS called the Target
2. Make a Damage Roll.
3. Select another figure in the Unit adjacent to the Target
4. Repeat 2 & 3 until there are no more Hits to allocate or else there are no more figures left in the Unit to select.

12.15.1 ALLOCATING HITS (1)

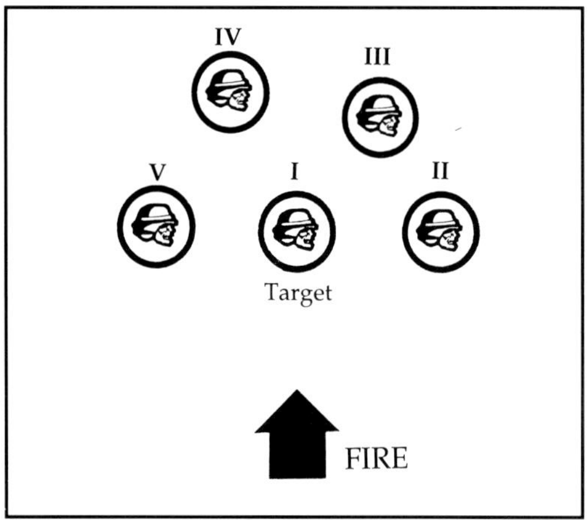

5. Select a figure in an adjacent Unit - though that figure must not be further than 70mm from the Target.
6. Repeat 2 - 5 until there are no more Hits to allocate.

12.15.2 ALLOCATING HITS (2)

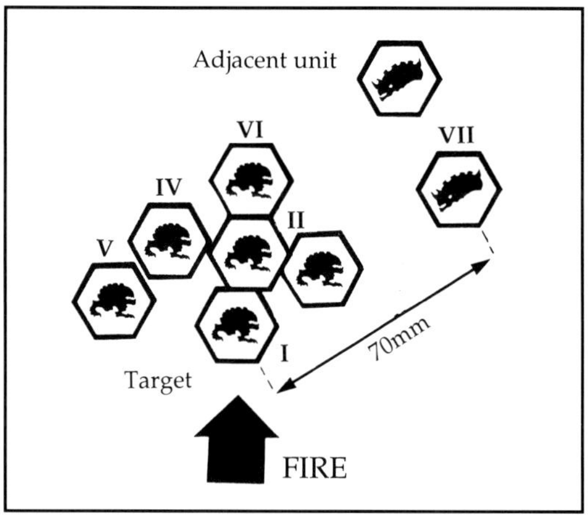

12.17. Area Effect Weapons

An AREA EFFECT Weapon is one whose effects are spread over a wide area. This effect is simulated by placing an AREA EFFECT TEMPLATE.

A Template is placed along the Line of Fire. DIRECTLY PLACED Area Effect Templates are put down touching the base of the firing figure.

When placed a Template is said to SHADOW a figure if its centre is Shadowed by any part of the Template or if the Template covers at least half the figure. A figure can be under more than one Template and if so will take damage from each one separately.

12.18. Targeting Rolls: Ranged Area Effect Weapons

Nominate a POINT OF AIM by placing a TARGETING COUNTER. Then the Range is measured to the Targeting Counter and normal procedures for firing are carried out. [see 12.12]

If the Targeting Roll falls in Zone E or F then the shot misses. [see 12.21]. Otherwise the shot is a Hit. Place the Range Template (for the weapon fired) Impact Point on the nominated point of impact.

Figures Shadowed by the Template make a Damage Roll modified by the Impact Modifier for that weapon. [see 14.1]

12.17 SPORE AREA EFFECT WEAPON

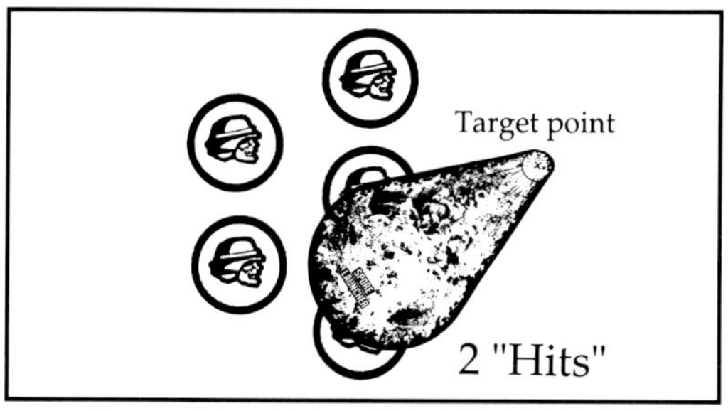

12.19. The Machine Cannon / Auto-Cannon Template

When firing a Machine Cannon, and after having determined the impact point, place the MACHINE CANNON TEMPLATE by:

(i) placing the first Burst Template on the Point of Impact.

(ii) roll one D10

(iii) position the arrow on the second Burst Template so that it points directly at the number on the first Template which corresponds to the number rolled on the die.

(iv) repeat (i) to (iii) to position the third Burst Template with relation to the second as the second was positioned relative to the first. Repeat this for the fourth and final Burst Template.

Figures Shadowed by the Template make a Damage Roll modified by the Impact Modifier for that weapon. [see 14.1]

12.18 USE OF MACHINE/AUTO CANNON TEMPLATES

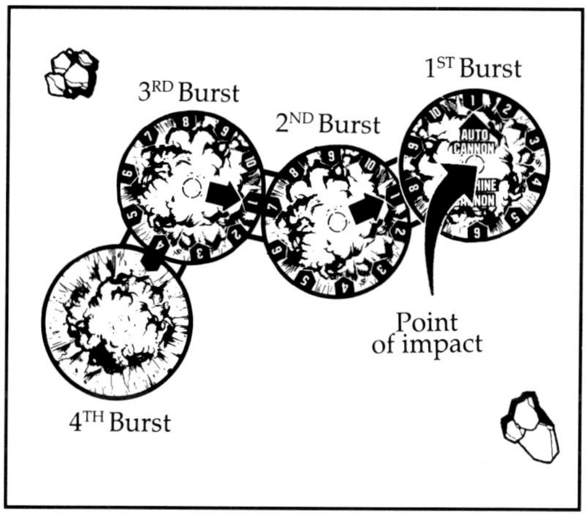

12.20. Use of the Cluster Missile Template

When firing a Cluster Missile, and after having determined the impact point, place the CLUSTER MISSILE TEMPLATE by:

(i) placing the first Burst Template on the Point of Impact.

(ii) roll two D10

(iii) position the arrows on the secondary Burst Templates so that they each point directly at a number on the first Template which corresponds to one of the numbers rolled on the die.

Figures Shadowed by the Template make a Damage Roll modified by the Impact Modifier for that weapon. [see 14.1]

12.19 USE OF CLUSTER MISSILE TEMPLATES

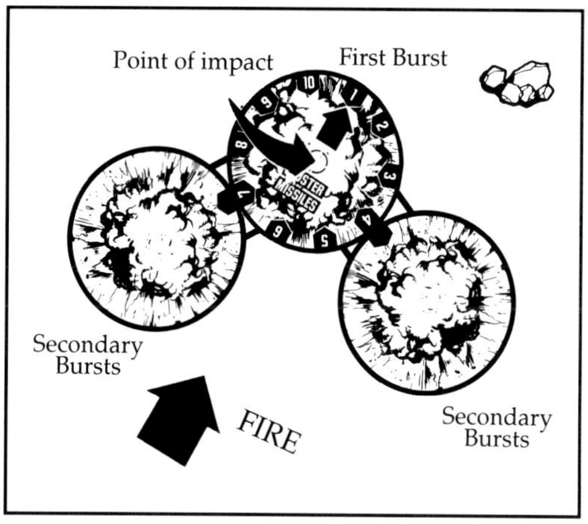

12.21. Deviation of Ranged Area Effect Weapons

The CIRCULAR DEVIATION TEMPLATE is used whenever a Ranged Area Effect Weapon misses.

Place the Template on the Point of Aim [see 12.18], with the 1 on the Template pointing towards the firing figure.

Roll one D10 to determine the Direction of Deviation. Then use the following to determine the Distance of Deviation:

Short:	1 D10 x 10mm
Medium:	2 D10 x 10mm
Long:	3 D10 x 10mm
Extreme:	4 D10 x 10mm

Measure this Distance of Deviation in the indicated Direction of Deviation and place the centre of the Burst Template there.

12.20 DEVIATION OF A RANGED AREA EFFECT WEAPON

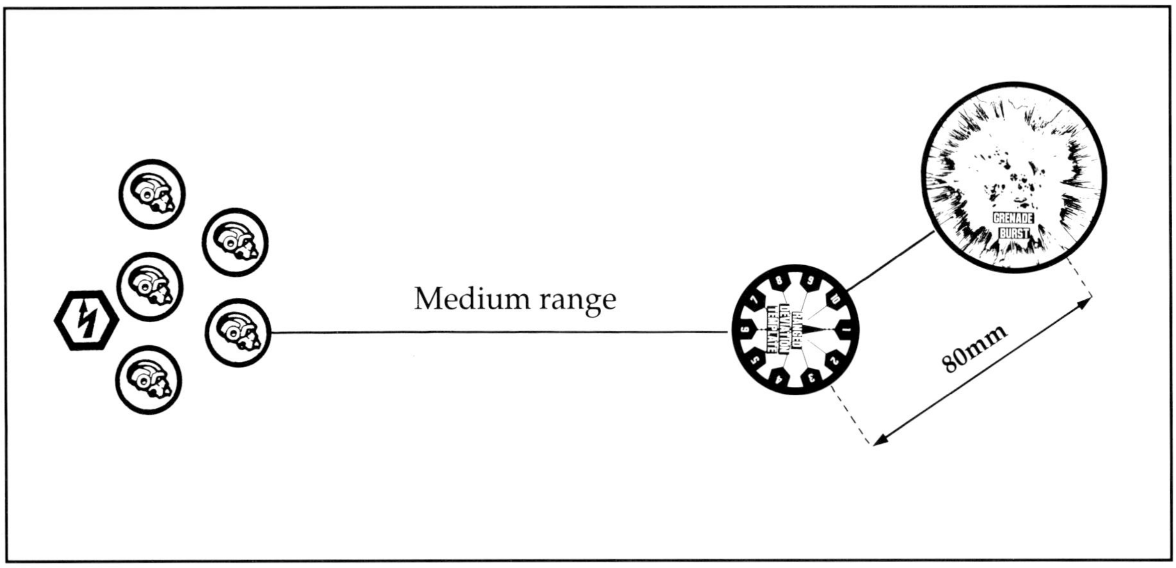

Example: SWATs fail a Targeting Roll at Medium Range with a grenade launcher. They roll a 10 for the Direction of Deviation and they throw a 5 and a 3 leading to a Distance of Deviation of 80mm. [see Diagram]

NOTE: ***The shot cannot deviate back into firer. If it does roll another D10 to determine a new Direction of Deviation.***

Figures Shadowed by the Template make a Damage Roll modified by the Impact Modifier for that weapon. [see 14.1]

If the Targeting Roll falls in Zones E or F then the shot deviates. [see 12.23]

12.21 WARRIOR USING BIO-ACID SPRAY

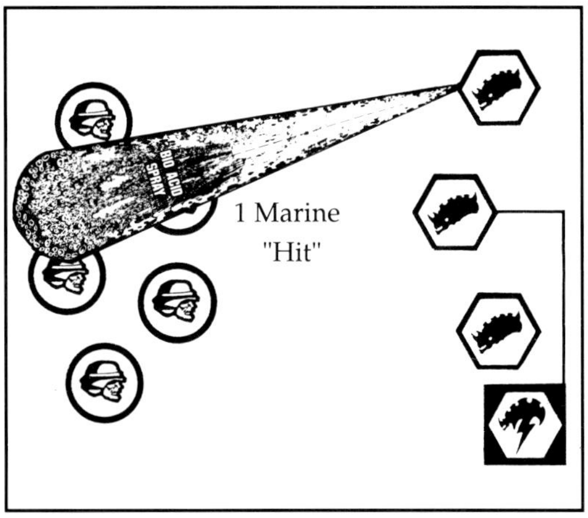

12.22. Targeting Roll: Directly Placed Area Effect Weapons.

Place the DIRECTLY PLACED AREA EFFECT TEMPLATE in the direction that the weapon is aimed (starting from the base of the figure).

Make a Targeting Roll using the raw Ranged Combat Ability for the firer without any Modifiers to determine the Rolling Column.

If the roll falls in Zone D or better of the Resolution Table [see 2] then the Template is left where it is.

Figures Shadowed by the Template make a Damage Roll modified by the Impact Modifier for that weapon. [see 14.1]

12.23. Deviation of Directly Placed Templates

The DIRECTLY PLACED DEVIATION TEMPLATE is used whenever a Direct Area Effect Weapon misses.

Place the Template in front of the figure and line up in the direction that the weapon was aimed.

Roll one D10 to determine the Angle of Deviation and put down the appropriate Direct Area Effect Template along this new direction.

12.22 DEVIATION OF A DIRECT PLACED AREA EFFECT WEAPON

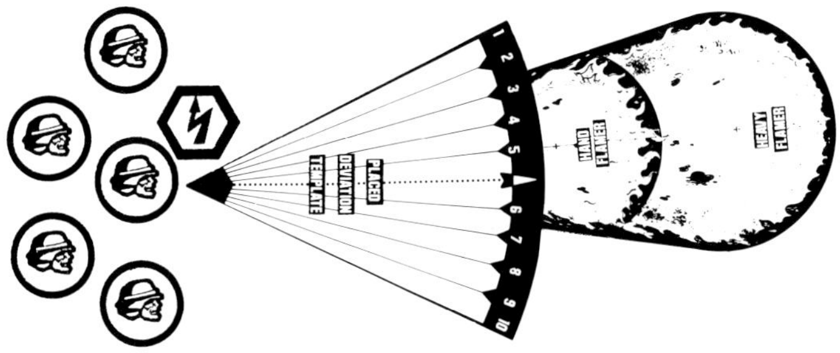

> Example: a Squad of Marines fail a Targeting Roll with a heavy flamer. They roll a D10 to determine the Angle of Deviation. The result is a 5. See diagram.

Figures Shadowed by the Template make a Damage Roll modified by the Impact Modifier for that weapon. [see 14.1]

12.24. Area Effect Weapons: Vehicles & Modules

In the event of a Vehicle or Module being targeted by an Area Effect Weapon two conditions will determine whether it will take a Damage Roll:

(i) the Template for the Area Effect Weapon must Shadow at least half of the Vehicle or Module.

(ii) at least half of the Template for the Area Effect Weapon must Shadow the Vehicle or Module.

12.25. Warmaster Vulnerability

If a Warmaster is within 70mm of a Group then it will count as being a member of that Group for targeting purposes.

A Warmaster that is raised to its full height presents a far easier target to enemy fire.

Close Combat

CLOSE COMBAT can only be initiated by a Charge Move. The Charging Unit merges fluidly with the target Unit so that potentially [see 13.9] all the figures in both Units can take part in the combat.

13.0.1 CLOSE COMBAT (1)

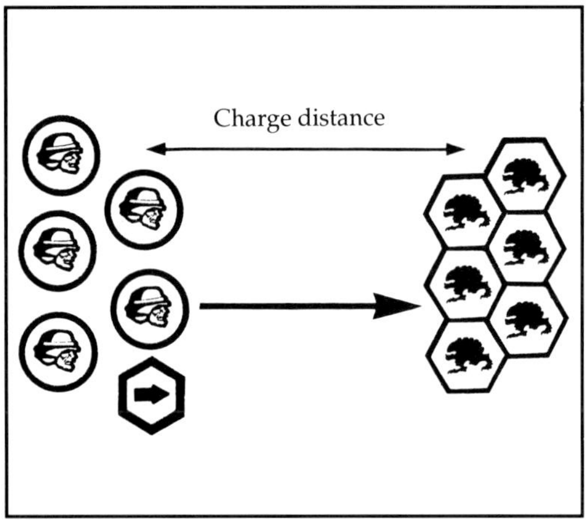

13.0.2 CLOSE COMBAT (2)

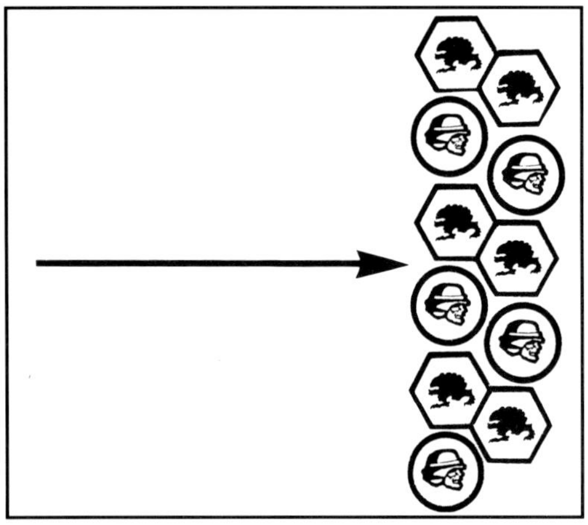

13.1. Close Combat Ability: Nexus

CLOSE COMBAT ABILITY reflects the proficiency that a Squad has in close combat.

Close Combat Ability for Nexus Human Troops is directly related to Experience Rating [see 5.3] as follows:

GREEN:	6	**ELITE :**	11
REGULAR:	8	**HELCAT:**	6
VETERAN:	10	**TALOS:**	10

NOTE: ***The Close Combat Ability is actually the Base Column Number for Close Combat. [see 2]***

NOTE: ***The Helcat is not designed for Close Combat.***

13.2. Close Combat Abilities: Kryomek

A Kryomek has a CLOSE COMBAT ABILITY which reflects its proficiency with weapons but also it has various Modifiers that represent its formidable, natural, somatic weapons that it can use even when it is 'unarmed'.

Different Castes of Kryomek can make a different number of 'unarmed attack'. Thus:

WARMASTER: 3 attacks (two arm strikes & one tail strike)

WARRIOR: 2 attacks (two arm strike)

HELION: 1 attack (general attack)

> Example: an unarmed Warmaster could use its tail strike and two arm strikes to attack three different targets simultaneously.

The various somatic weapons for the different Castes have associated Strike and Impact Modifiers:

	Strike	Impact
Warmaster Arm Strike:	0	+2
Warmaster Tail Strike:	-2	+3
Warrior Arm Strike:	0	+1
Helion:	0	+3

In Close Combat a Kryomek can use weapons in addition to some of its natural abilities. Clearly it loses 1 arm strike for each weapon that it is using (and sometimes 2 for larger weapons).

Example: an unarmed Warrior could make two arm strikes. A Warrior armed with a single-molecule blade could make only one arm strike as well as using the blade. A Warrior armed with a corroder lance can make no arm strikes.

A Kryomek has a Close Combat Ability related to its Caste:

WARMASTER: 15

WARRIOR: 12

HELION: 9

NOTE: The Close Combat Ability is actually the Base Column Number for Close Combat. [see 2]

13.3. Rolling Columns: Close Combat

Close Combat is determined by means of a STRIKE ROLL made on an appropriate Rolling Column.

To determine the Rolling Column [see 2.1] for a weapon in Close Combat take the Close Combat Ability for the figure fighting and add the weapon's Strike Modifier.

Units in Close Combat are always assumed to be Motivated.

13.4. Strike Rolls

Having determined the Rolling Column the Strike Roll is made by rolling one D20 to determine the result on the Resolution Table. [see 2.2].

The actual result does depend a lot on the RANK of the weapon:

Rank 1

The result depends in which Zone of the Resolution Table the roll lands:

Zones E & F: a miss

Other Zones: cause 1 hit.

Rank 2

The result depends in which Zone of the Resolution Table the roll lands:

Zones E & F: a miss

Zones C & D: cause 1 Hit

Zones A & B: cause 2 Hits

Rank 3

The result depends in which Zone of the Resolution Table the roll lands:

Zones E & F: a miss

Zone D: causes 1 hit.

Zones B & C: cause 2 hits.

Zone A: causes 3 hits.

13.5. Allocating Hits

When a Unit Charges into a Close Combat each figure in the Unit is allocated a single opponent figure in the enemy Unit. This is done on a one-to-one basis. Any figures left over (ie. figures in the more numerous Unit that have no opponents allocated) begin the whole process again until every figure in the Combat has an opponent.

NOTE: ***When allocating more than one opponent to a figure the relative sizes of the combatants should be taken into account. [see 13.9]***

13.6. Winning a Close Combat

This is defined as a Unit inflicting more casualties in total than it received in total in a Close Combat.

If the defeated Unit is Pushed Back or goes into Panic then the victorious Unit if it is a Squad can take a Resistance Test if it does not wish to Follow Up or Pursue it. [see 8.5]

13.7. Losing a Close Combat

This is defined as a Unit taking more casualties in total than those it has inflicted in total in a Close Combat.

Such a Unit if it is a Squad must take a Resistance Test which might result in it being Pushed Back or Panicking. [see 8.5]

13.8. Swarming

On a battlefield Helions may form a SWARM MASS. This is a dense formation which only has the frontage of a Helion Group.

Any number of Helion Groups can merge behind another forming a column or Mass. The entire Mass must have a frontage no greater than the leading Group and must maintain Cohesion [see 5.8]. The whole of the Swarm Mass can then be Activated and Controlled by a Warmaster as one body.

To Charge place the Control Counters for all the Groups behind the Swarm Mass in a stack. The Warmaster can then Activate the Mass 'en masse'.

13.8.1 HELIONS SWARMING

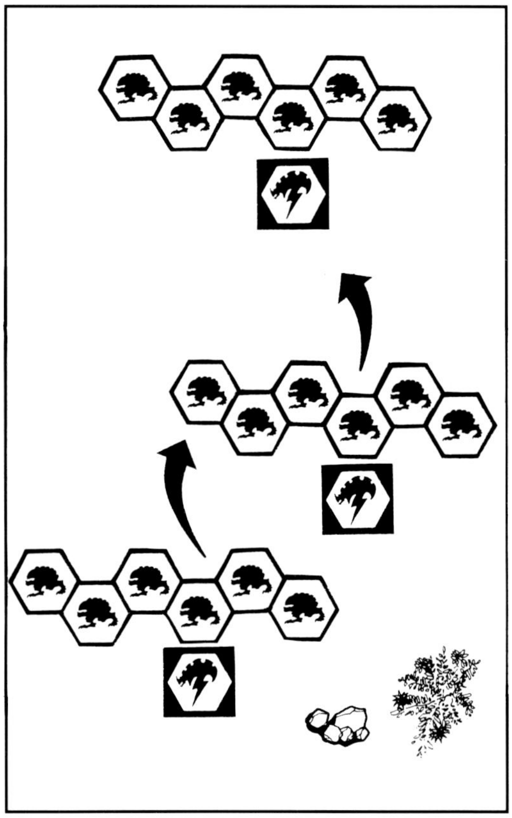

13.8.2 SWARM MASS

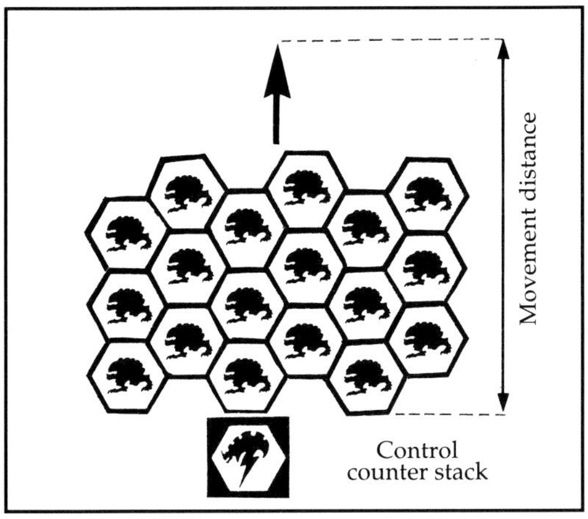

13.9. Size

The SIZE of a creature is a relative measure of it bulk. Thus a:

HUMAN: is of Size 3

CBU: is of Size 3

HELION: is of Size 3

WARRIOR: is of Size 5

WARMASTER: is of Size 6

13.10. Using the Relative Size Table

The RELATIVE SIZE TABLE is used to simulate the fact that because of its Size [see 13.9] it might be possible for more than one attacker to engage a creature.

The following relates the procedure for using the Relative Size Table:

(i) move down left hand column of the Table until a row is found corresponding to the attacker's Size

(ii) move along the top of the Table until a column is found corresponding to the defender's Size.

(iii) the intersection of this row and column contains a value which is the maximum number of attackers that can engage a defender of that Size.

13.11. Relative Size Table

	1	2	3	4	5	6	7	8	9	10
1	4	5	6	7	8	9	10	11	12	13
2	3	4	5	6	7	8	9	10	11	12
3	2	3	4	5	6	7	8	9	10	11
4	1	2	3	4	5	6	7	8	9	10
5	1	1	2	3	4	5	6	7	8	9
6	1	1	1	2	3	4	5	6	7	8
7	1	1	1	1	2	3	4	5	6	7
8	1	1	1	1	1	2	3	4	5	6
9	1	1	1	1	1	1	2	3	4	5
10	1	1	1	1	1	1	1	2	3	4

Example: 15 Helions (Size 3) charge into a Close Combat against 3 Nexus Marines (Size 3). Using the Table it is determined that a maximum of 4 Helions can engage any one man. Therefore 12 Helions could fight in total.

13.12. Firing into a Close Combat

Weapons that are fired into a Close Combat will have a certain chance of hitting any figure taking part in that combat.

All Area Effect Weapons are handled in the standard way for that weapon. [ie. any figure under the appropriate template will have a chance of being hit.]

Vehicles in a Close Combat can act as Obstacles and will block LOS. [see 11.1]

13.12 FIRING INTO COMBAT

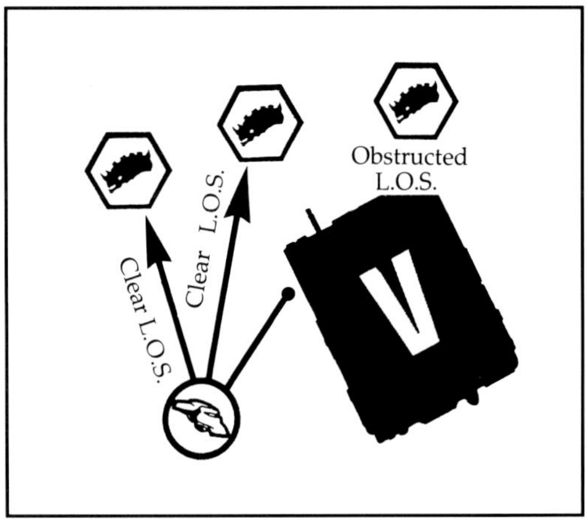

Direct Fire Weapons are treated in the standard way up to the point where hits are being allocated [see 12.16] when it will have to be determined if friendly Units have been hit.

The chance of friendly Units being hit depends on how the TOTAL SIZE of all the figures comprising them compares with the Total Size of all unfriendly Units taking part in the combat.

The Total Size of a body of figures is the sum of all the Sizes for each of them. [see 13.9]

The following relates the procedure for using the Comparison Table:

(i) move down left hand column of the Table until a row is found corresponding to the Total Size of all the friendly figures

(ii) move along the top of the Table until a column is found corresponding to the Total Size of all the unfriendly figures

(iii) the intersection of this row and column contains a value. A D20 is rolled - if this is lower than or equal to this value then a friendly figure has been hit.

Damage is calculated as before.

Example 1 - six Helions fighting three marines being fired on by a Unit of marines. Helions and marines are both Size 3.

Helion Total Size 3x6=18

Marine Total Size 3x3=9

therefore Helion Total Size is greater than the marines Total Size in the ratio 2:1.

Example 2: three Warriors fighting against three SWAT team being fired upon by marines.

Warriors Total Size 3x5=15

SWAT Total Size 3x3=9

The ratio here is 9:15 (which is divided by 3 to bring it within the limits of the Comparison Table ie. 3:5)

Referencing this against the Comparison Table yields a result of 7. One D20 is thrown and if it is less than 7 then the Marines hit the SWATs.

13.13. Comparison Table

D20	1	2	3	4	5	6	7	8	9	10
1	10	7	5	4	3	3	3	2	2	2
2	13	10	8	7	6	5	4	4	4	3
3	15	12	10	8	7	7	6	5	5	5
4	16	13	12	10	9	8	7	7	6	6
5	16	14	12	11	10	9	8	8	7	7
6	17	15	13	12	11	10	9	9	8	7
7	17	16	14	13	12	11	10	9	9	8
8	18	16	14	13	12	11	11	10	9	9
9	18	16	15	14	13	12	11	11	10	9
10	18	17	15	14	13	12	11	11	10	10

13.14. Vehicles in Close Combat

Some Vehicles are armed with weapons that can be brought to bear in a Close Combat. Some Striders however can also carry out a Stomp Attack. [see 13.15]

13.15. Stomp Attacks

Hajunka Storm Striders are capable of delivering a Close Combat STOMP ATTACK. (This is a feature built into the MOA BBC mk II series biped chassis.) [see Hardware]

The Stomp Attack is treated like any other Close Combat Weapon and has an effective Close Combat Ability of 7. [see Hardware]

Damage

Humans and Helions are frail creatures. The deadly, advanced weapons of the 35th Century and the terrifying weapons of the Kryomeks rarely inflict recoverable wounds. To simulate this Humans and Helions are never wounded - any damage sustained is fatal.

14.1. The Damage Roll

Take the Defender's Armour Class and add to it the Impact Modifier to get the Rolling Column.

Having determined the Rolling Column one D20 is rolled to determine the resulting damage on the Resolution Table. [see 2.2]. This resulting damage depends in which Zone of the Resolution Table the roll lands and the nature of the target.

All rolls landing in either Zone E or Zone F cause no damage.

In situations where the damage called for has already been received then the next lesser damage condition is applied.

14.2. Damage to CBUs

Having made a Damage Roll the result depends in which Zone of the Resolution Table the roll falls:

Zone A-C: the CBU is destroyed.

Zone D: the CBU is damaged. Roll one D10 to determine the consequences:

- **1-2** propulsion system is damaged - CBU immobilised.
- **3-4** primary weapons destroyed.
- **5-6** forced rechanneling of micro-circuits. Place one KO Counter beside CBU.
- **7-8** forced rechanneling of micro-circuits. Place two KO Counters beside CBU.
- **9-10** cyberneural damage - CBU will fire on or engage closest Unit whether friendly or not.

NOTE: ***a CBU with a KO Counter beside it is considered inoperative.***

14.3. Damage to Vehicles

Vehicles and their systems can suffer damage from a wide variety of sources. The most obvious are direct impact damage but even the intrusion of fine dust particles can clog weapon mountings and cause electronic surface degradation.

Having made a Damage Roll [see 14.1] the result depends in which Zone of the Resolution Table the roll falls:

Zone A: the Vehicle is destroyed. Roll one D10 to determine the consequences for its Crew:

- **1-4** Crew escape and form new Squad.
- **5-7** roll D10 for each Crew member: 1-5 Crew member escapes; 6-10 Crew member is killed.
- **8-10** Crew killed

NOTE: ***escaped Crews have to make an immediate Resistance Test to stop them going into Panic.***

Zone B-D: the Vehicle is damaged.

Roll one D10 to determine the consequences:

- **1-2** propulsion damage - 1/2 speed. Reduce Handling Class by two.
- **3-5** one of its Secondary Weapons is destroyed.
- **6-8** one of its Primary Weapons is destroyed.
- **9-10** immobilised though the weaponry is still functional.

14.4. Damage to Battlefront Modules

BATTLEFRONT MODULES [see 15] consist of MODULAR UNITS such as DOMES, BUNKERS and CORRIDORS often linked together to form a COMPLEX.

Each Modular Unit is a separate target and is treated as a Vehicle. Squads inside a Module are treated as if they were that 'Vehicle's' Crew.

A standard Targeting or Strike Roll is made and the result depends in which Zone the Roll falls:

Zone D: Little Damage - though if the target is a Corridor it s blocked.

Zones B & C: Minor Damage - roll one D10:

- **8-10** Armour Class reduced by 1
- **5-7** one Secondary Function destroyed
- **1-4** one Primary Function destroyed

Zone A: Major Damage - roll one D10:

- **7-10** Crew escape but primary and secondary functions destroyed
- **4-6** Module destroyed and 50% of Crew killed
- **1-3** Module destroyed and all the Crew killed

14.5. Damage to Warriors

Having made a Damage Roll [see14.1] the result depends in which Zone of the Resolution Table the roll falls:

Zones E & F: cause no damage.

Zone D: causes a WOUND.

Zones A-C: a KILL.

A Wounded Warrior will go 'shell down' and will not fire any weapons. It will however attack and engage in Close Combat any enemy Unit that comes within 40mm of it.

14.6. Damage to Warmasters

Because of their special resilience Warmasters have to be treated separately.

After making the standard Damage Roll [see 14.1] the result is determined as follows:

Zones E & F: no damage

Zone D: causes a WOUND & loss of 1 CV

Zone C: causes a WOUND & loss of 2 CV

Zone B: causes a WOUND & loss of 3 CV

Zone A: a KILL

NOTE: ***A Warmaster suffers no negative effects from being Wounded except for a loss of Control Counters.***

14.7. Squad & Group Cohesion - Casualties

In Phase 6 casualties might have caused some Squads and Groups to lose Cohesion [see 5.5 & 5.8]. The Unit must be made Cohesive by moving as few figures as possible. Figures must be moved the minimum distance possible so that the Unit *just* achieves Cohesion.

If a Squad Leader is killed then a new one must be nominated and the rest of the Squad regrouped around him.

14.8. Vehicle Collisions

When a Vehicle collides with another Object (Vehicle, Building or Terrain Feature / Obstacle ect) then compare the mass of the two Objects.

Object A has a greater mass than Object B. If the difference between them is:

0-4 then A and B are brought to a stand still if they are not already so. Both take damage as if they had taken a Damage Roll on the Resolution Table and it had landed in Zones B-D. Ignore the damage to either Object if it is a terrain feature.

5-9 B takes damage as if it had taken a Damage Roll on the Resolution Table and it had landed in Zones B-D. When the D10 is rolled for the consequences of the damage a modifier is applied to the roll which is equal to the Speed Bands of A and B added together. If B is a terrain feature it is destroyed - otherwise it is thrown to one side. Use the Ranged Deviation Template to determine the direction.

A is unharmed and its Speed Band is immediately reduced by one.

10 + B takes damage as if it had taken a Damage Roll on the Resolution Table and it had landed in Zone A. If B is a terrain feature it is destroyed - otherwise it is thrown to one side. Use the Ranged Deviation Template to determine the direction.

A is completely unharmed and its movement is unaffected.

Environment

The term ENVIRONMENT is applied to any landform, artifact natural or artificial or any other object that is a to be considered as part of the environment - even if only for the duration of the current game.

15.1. Environment

There are three types of Environment:

(i) TERRAIN.

(ii) OBSTACLES.

(iii) BATTLEFRONT MODULES

15.2. Terrain

Terrain is broken down into FIVE categories:

A GOOD TERRAIN

fairly flat/moon surface

low terrain elevations

undulating ground

etc

B VEHICLE-BAD TERRAIN

high gradient terrain elevations

dense foliage / jungle

xeno-arbiforms / alien macro-vegetation

C INFANTRY-BAD TERRAIN

sandy/very soft

shallow water or other fluid expanse

high gradient terrain elevations

dense foliage / jungle

xeno-arbiforms / alien macro-vegetation

D VEHICLE-IMPASSABLE TERRAIN

vertical cliffs

etc

E INFANTRY-IMPASSABLE TERRAIN

vertical cliffs

ravines / canyons

etc

15.3. Bad Terrain

Generally because of the extremely varied nature of terrain forms and the equally diverse Unit and Vehicle types the effects that a particular terrain has on a Unit can not be fully determined. To some extent this has to be left to mutual agreement by the players before the game begins. [see 4.2]

15.4. Obstacles

OBSTACLES are Environmental features (such as large rocks, large plant forms, pieces of wreckage etc) which can cause damage to Vehicles and provide Cover [see Cover..]. An Obstacle will only cause damage to a Vehicle that collides with it. [see Collision]

15.5. Vehicle-Bad Terrain

The Crew of any Vehicle entering or travelling through Vehicle-Bad Terrain at speeds greater than Speed Band 1 must take a Resistance Test to see if they can maintain control of their Vehicle.

If the Crew fails the Resistance Test then they are assumed to have lost control of the Vehicle and they take damage as if they had taken a Damage Roll on the Resolution Table and it had landed in Zones B-D. When the D10 is rolled for the consequences of the damage a Modifier is applied to the roll which is equal to the number of Speed Bands above 1 that the Vehicle is travelling at. Additionally the Vehicle immediately has its speed reduced to Speed Band 1.

15.6. Infantry-Bad Terrain

Squads, Groups and CBUs are forced to reduce their speed by half when entering or crossing Infantry-Bad terrain.

15.7. Combinations of Terrain Types

A piece of terrain can be both Vehicle and Infantry-Bad Terrain - and will affect both accordingly.

15.8. Vehicle-Impassable Terrain

A Vehicle moving into Vehicle-Impassable Terrain takes damage as if it had taken a Damage Roll on the Resolution Table and it had landed in Zone B-D. When the D10 is rolled for the consequences of the damage a modifier is applied equal to the Speed Band at which it is travelling.

15.9. Infantry-Impassable Terrain

Squads, Groups and CBUs cannot enter Infantry-Impassable Terrain.

CHAPTER 10

HARDWARE

Desk Split File View Update Visc MultiTaskWOS v8.2.1

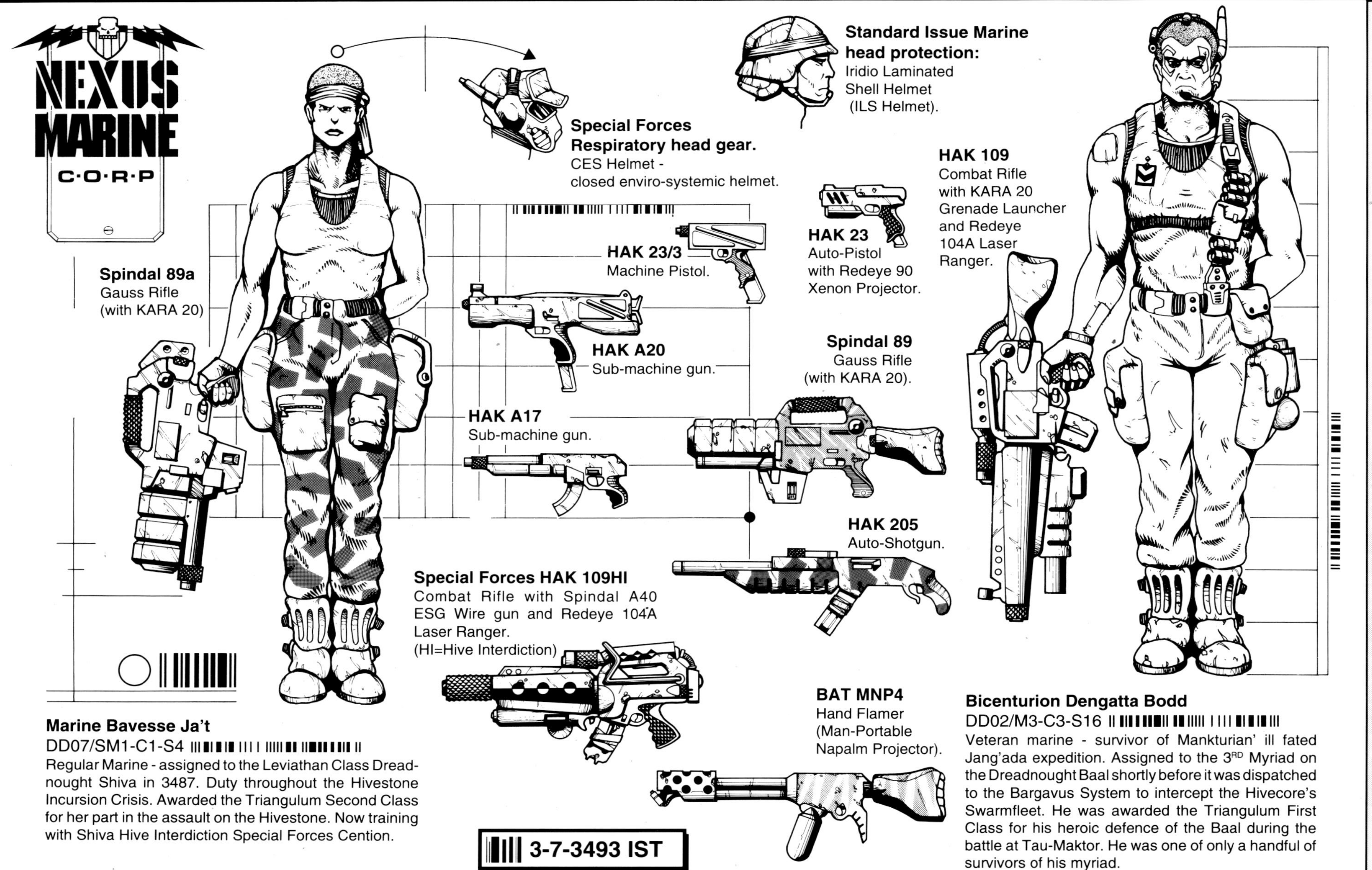

Marine Bavesse Ja't

DD07/SM1-C1-S4

Regular Marine - assigned to the Leviathan Class Dreadnought Shiva in 3487. Duty throughout the Hivestone Incursion Crisis. Awarded the Triangulum Second Class for her part in the assault on the Hivestone. Now training with Shiva Hive Interdiction Special Forces Cention.

Bicenturion Dengatta Bodd

DD02/M3-C3-S16

Veteran marine - survivor of Mankturian' ill fated Jang'ada expedition. Assigned to the 3RD Myriad on the Dreadnought Baal shortly before it was dispatched to the Bargavus System to intercept the Hivecore's Swarmfleet. He was awarded the Triangulum First Class for his heroic defence of the Baal during the battle at Tau-Maktor. He was one of only a handful of survivors of his myriad.

3-7-3493 IST

Input Media

Nexus Troops

Nexus troops can be broken down into three broad categories:

MARINES: the standard, mainstream backbone of all Nexus ground forces. Equipped with a wide range of Nexus personnel weapons and armour, however greens would never be equipped with power-armour.

SHOCK: The Elite units formed from the cream of the standard forces. Supplied with state-of-the-art weaponry and armour.

CYCLOS: Convict Special Forces - the cannon-fodder - armed with dangerous but powerful equipment - little protective gear.

EXP Rating	RC	CC	ML
Elite	11	11	16
Veteran	10	10	14
Regular	8	8	12
Green	6	6	10

Personnel Armours (Soft)	AC
Unarmoured man	10
Laminated Plasticated Weave	9
Light Battle Suits	8
Battle Suits	7
Power Armour	5
Crystallated Beryllium Bronze	4

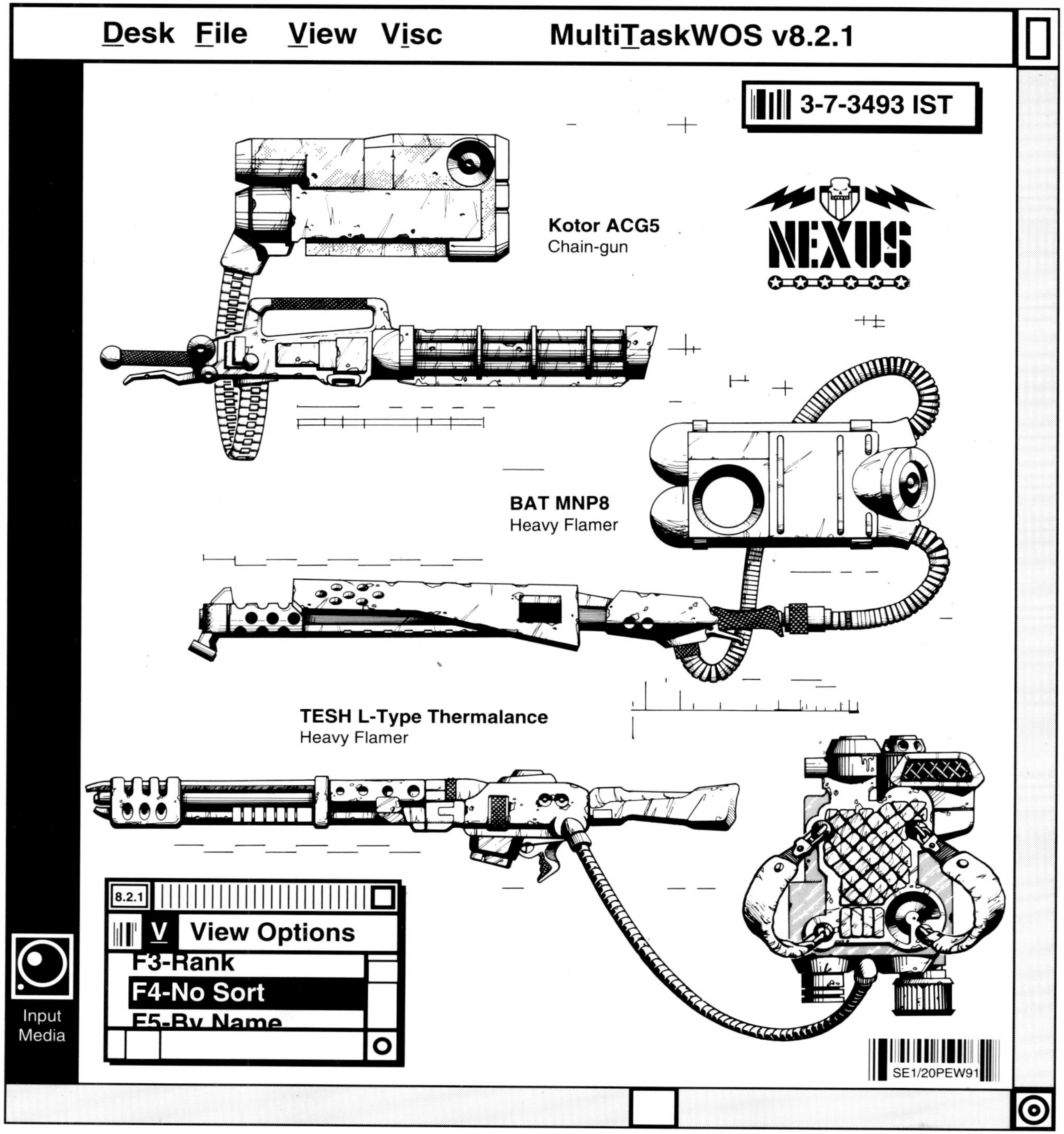

Desk File View Visc MultiTaskWOS v8.2.1

3-7-3493 IST

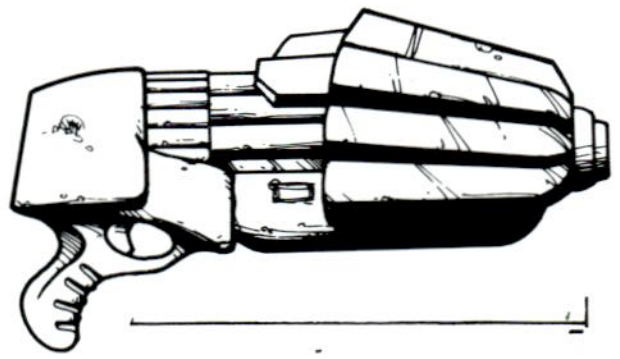

Spindal 120
Gauss rifle with inbuilt gyroscopics for one-handed use in Close Combat and heavy electro-mag baffling for stealth operations.

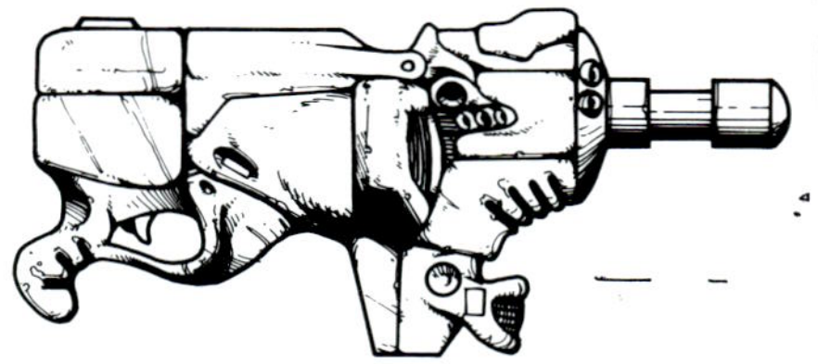

Hardon & Kluvis Reflex Rifle
State of the art combat rifle with motion trackers, passive range-finding and full stealth baffling (imperceptible reaction on firing). Reflex gyroscopics allow one-handed use and target tracking in Close Combat.

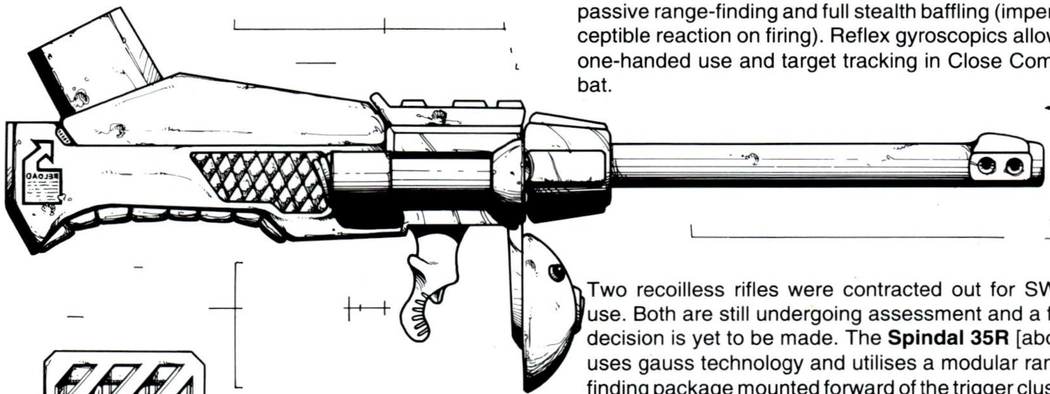

Two recoilless rifles were contracted out for SWAT use. Both are still undergoing assessment and a final decision is yet to be made. The **Spindal 35R** [above] uses gauss technology and utilises a modular range-finding package mounted forward of the trigger cluster. The **HAK 320** [below] uses conventional propulsion and thus has a better rate of fire and is lighter.

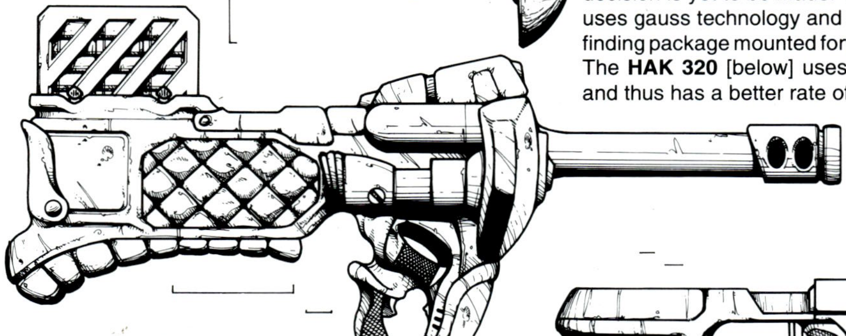

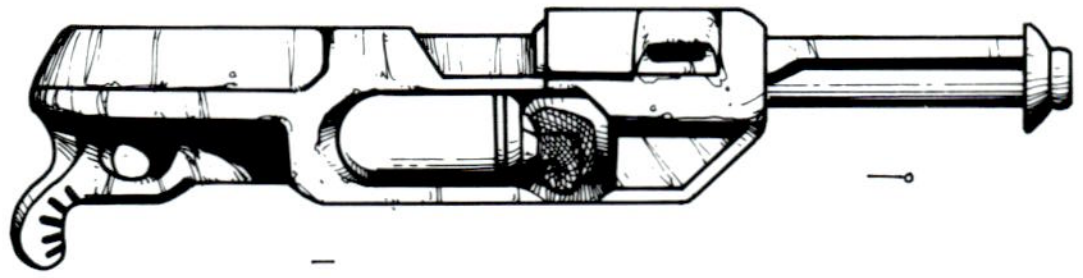

BAT MNP -Special is a modification of the BAT MNP4 used by Regular NTFA forces. It is lighter and more reliable.

Input Media

Weapon Descriptions

AUTO-PISTOL
Small repeating pistol. Fires 5mm rounds.

MACHINE PISTOL
Small, rapid fire, pistol sized machine gun. Fires 5mm rounds.

SUB MACHINE GUN
Short, rapid fire rifle. Fires 3mm caseless rounds in three round or full auto bursts.

COMBAT RIFLE
Standard automatic rifle. Fires 2mm fin-stabilised, caseless darts in bursts of five. The ammo alternates between "Riprounds" that fragment on impact, and "Hardrounds" for SOFT armour penetration.

AUTO-SHOTGUN
Rapid fire, automatic feed shotgun. Each cartridge contains both mono-crystallic pellets and molecule-filament splinters.

XENOPROD
Telescoping, pump-action Close Combat weapon. The primed cartridge is housed in the far end of the prod and is detonated when any of the pressure triggers at the end of the rod are depressed.

LIGHT MACHINE GUN
A combat rifle with upgraded ammo feed rate, improved range and belt-fed from an ammo hopper.

CHAIN-GUN
Rapid fire, high calibre weapon. The chain-gun has multiple barrels which rotate to enhance rate of fire and prolong sustained fire without over-heating. It fires alternating HI-Explosive and "Riprounds".

RECOILLESS RIFLE
A repeating, large calibre rifle fired from the shoulder. The ammo has an armour piercing central core surrounded by a splintering sabot for efficiency against SOFT and HARD armour types.

GRENADE LAUNCHER

Fires grenades from a repeating magazine.

GAUSS RIFLE

Uses pulsed magnetic fields to accelerate microscopic needles to extremely high velocities. It fires bursts of hundreds of needles in a fraction of a second. The rear section of each needle splinters to form an "umbrella" of molecular-filaments for maximum damage against "organics", while incorporating a dense mono-crystallic head for penetration of SOFT armour types.

HEAVY FLAMER

Muscilated Isoton-napalm dispenser with backpack ammo storage.

LIGHT FLAMER

Rifle sized Muscilated Isoton-napalm dispenser with a pressurised canister.

GYRO-MOUNT

A servo assisted harness that spreads weapon load for greater ease of movement and stabilisation while the firer is moving.

GAUSS CANNON

Heavier version of the Gauss Rifle.

SELF-GUIDED MISSILE

A fire-and-forget smart missile system for specific targetting of large targets.

NAPALM CANNON

Fires a delivery canister containing muscilated isoton-napalm. Each canister has a programmed longevity (automatically downloaded from the range-finding systems) which enables projection of its payload forward of a given point, whether impact has occurred or not. This weapon is either vehicular or modular mounted.

CHAIN CANNON

Higher calibre version of the Chain-Gun. This weapon is either vehicular or modular mounted.

Desk File View Visc MultiTaskWOS v8.2.1

YAG 500 - Special Forces Urban Interdiction Suit. Light PA

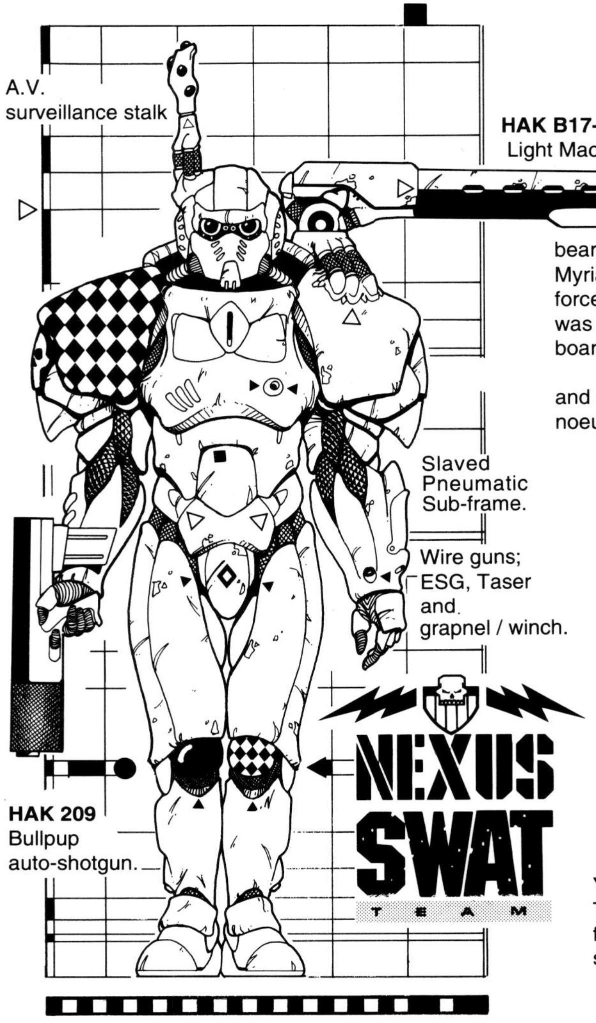

Although designed for Urban conflict, this suit bears the insignia of the Dreadnought Qatar's VacDef Myriad. The Qatar is the first Dreadnought to have such a force after the lessons learnt at Tau-Maktor when the Baal was almost overrun and the Astarte lost to Kryomek boarding actions.

The heavy shoulder padding protects the neck and shoulder areas from the various dismembering manoeuvres common to close combat with Kryomek.

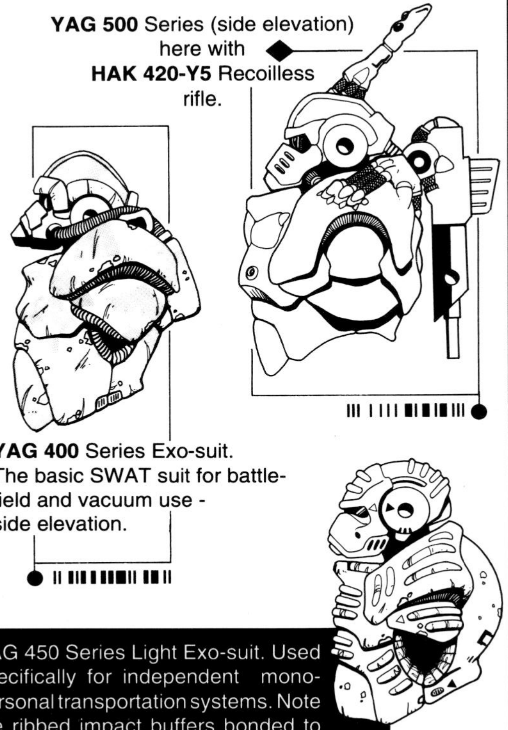

YAG 500 Series (side elevation) here with **HAK 420-Y5** Recoilless rifle.

YAG 400 Series Exo-suit. The basic SWAT suit for battlefield and vacuum use - side elevation.

YAG 450 Series Light Exo-suit. Used specifically for independent mono-personal transportation systems. Note the ribbed impact buffers bonded to the surface.

The Slaved Shoulder Mounted ordnance is used when halted and rarely utilised on the move, it provides covering fire within a binary unit (two-man "buddy" unit) used in interdiction operations.

This suit also proved effective in Hive penetration operations.

Input
Media

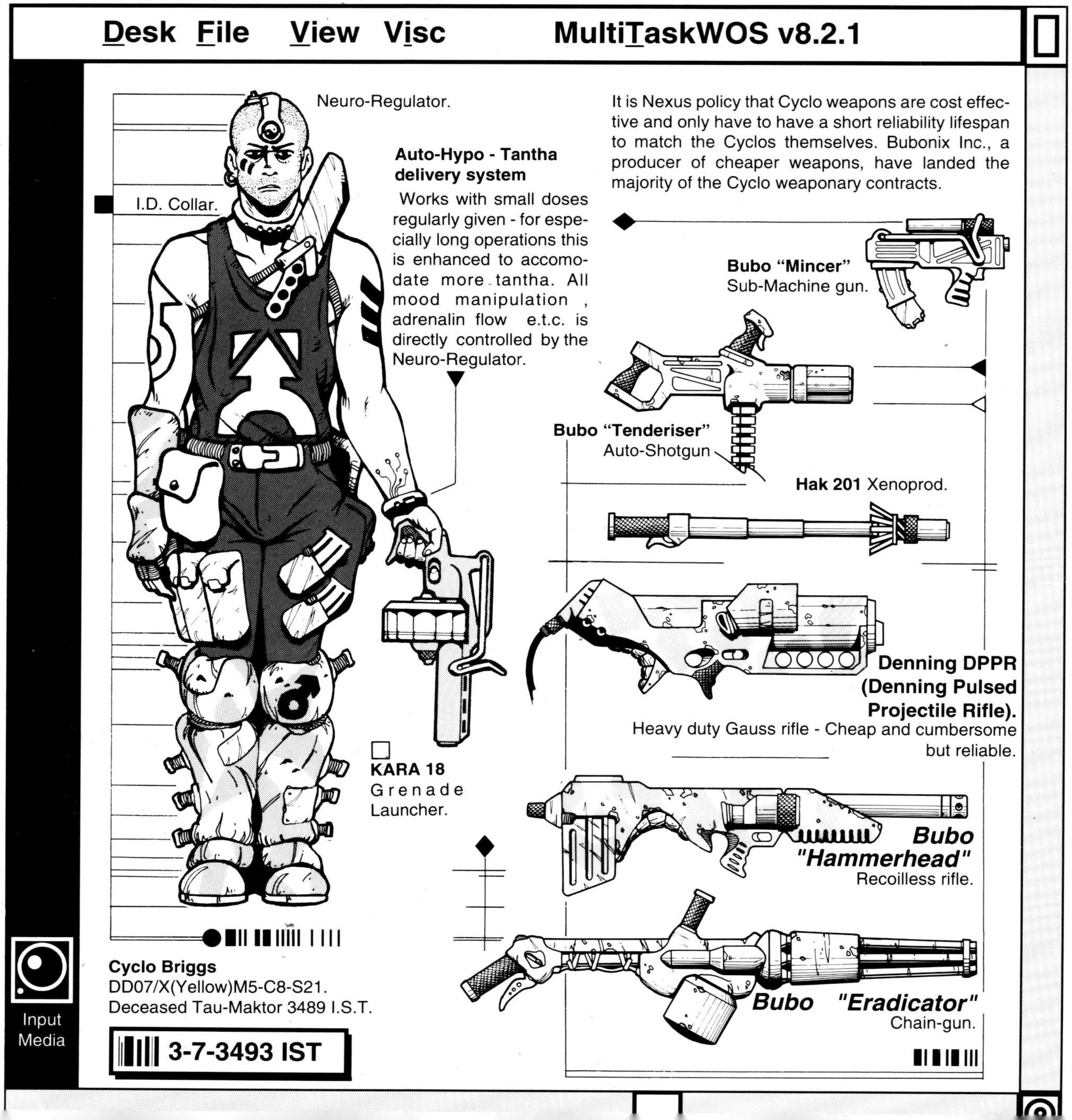

MACHINE CANNON

Smaller version of the Auto-Cannon. Fires bursts of HI-Explosive or armour piercing shells. This weapon is either vehicular or modular mounted.

CLUSTER MISSILES

Multi-Launch Rocket System. It fires a burst of missiles which splinter and bombard an area with a multitude of anti-personnel and anti-armour ordnance. The launcher is fed by a magazine housed within the vehicle or module.

HOWITZER

Huge calibre, multiple payload, area saturation gun. It fires programmed longevity canisters which splinter and bombard an area with a multitude of anti-personnel and anti-armour ordnance. This weapon is either vehicular or modular mounted.

CANNON

High calibre, single-shot, anti-armour shells. This weapon is either vehicular or modular mounted.

AUTO-CANNON

Ordnance that fires bursts of HI-Explosive anti-armour shells. This weapon is either vehicular or modular mounted.

Armoured Vehicles

Until recently the bulk of battlefield armoured vehicles consisted of traditional designs using conventional transport technologies. Bipedal vehicles have assumed many of these roles and are rapidly proving their greater flexibility on the battlefield.

Standard Armoured Vehicle Chassis & Hulls

There are three basic armoured vehicle chassis types commonly in use. These provide stable weapon platforms and use the commonly available transport technologies: wheeled (KAGA mk XIV-e W-Chassis), tracked (KAGA mk XXII-d T-Chassis) or hover (KAGA mk IX-n H-Chassis). The basic chassis is combined with a number of hull designs each performing a different battlefield function to produce a range of battlefield vehicles.

The manufacturer of these vehicles is KAGA Construction which is now a subsidiary of the Megacorp Hajunka.

There are a number of hull designs:

KAGA mk XII-3s Assault Gun

Mass:	**20**
Size:	**14**
Crew:	**3**
Armour:	**80mm iridio-steel (AC 4 - Hard)**
Primary Weapon:	**1 hull fixed mounted HAK 2000 Howitzer.**
Secondary Weapon:	**1 hull mounted HAK B17fm Light Machine Gun with a 45° Fire Arc.**

KAGA mk IV-4b APC

Mass:	**17**
Size:	**14**
Crew:	**2**
Armour:	**20mm iridio-steel (AC 13 - Hard)**
Armament:	**Small turret twin mounted Kotor ACG5 Chain-Gun. Restricted Arc of Fire (see model).**
Extra Crew Capacity:	**5**

KAGA mk X-2 Battletank

Mass:	**19**
Size:	**14**
Crew:	**3**
Armour:	**60mm iridio-steel (AC 7 - Hard)**
Primary Weapon:	**Turret mounted HAK 1010 Cannon with unrestricted Fire Arc.**
Secondary Weapon:	**1 hull mounted HAK B17fm Light Machine Gun with a 45° Fire Arc.**

KAGA mk VIII-11e Rocket Launcher

Mass:	**18**
Size:	**14**
Crew:	**2**
Armour:	**40mm iridio-steel (AC 10 - Hard)**
Primary Weapon:	**twin turret mounted Vector 12 "V12" Missile System with unrestricted Fire Arc.**
Secondary Weapon:	**1 hull mounted HAK B17fm Light Machine Gun with a 45° Fire Arc.**

Battlefield Assault Guns

Used as heavy anti-personnel battlefield mobile howitzers.

Ogre 234 Assault Gun

Hull Type:	**KAGA mk XII-3s**
Chassis Type:	**Wheeled KAGA mk XIV-e**
Handling Class:	**2**
Top Speed Band:	**Speed Band 2**
Max. Speed:	**240mm /turn**
Acceleration:	**1**
Deceleration:	**2**

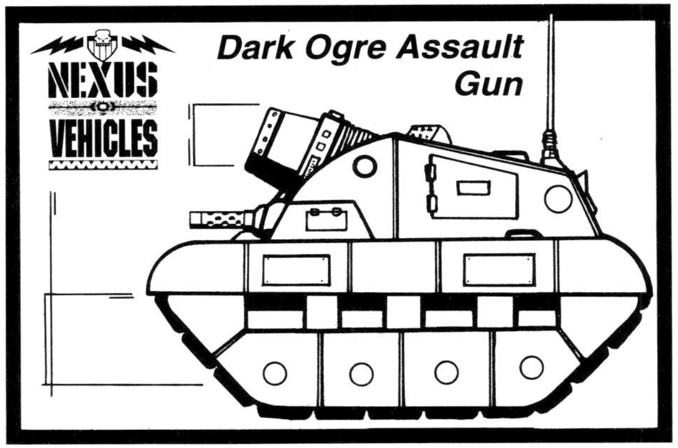

Darkogre Assault Gun

Hull Type:	KAGA mk XII-3s
Chassis Type:	Tracked KAGA mk XXII-d
Handling Class:	2
Top Speed Band:	Speed Band 2
Max. Speed:	240mm /turn
Acceleration:	1
Deceleration:	2

Cloud-Ogre 2

Hull Type:	KAGA mk XII-3s
Chassis Type:	Hover KAGA mk IX-n
Handling Class:	1
Top Speed Band:	Speed Band 2
Max. Speed:	240mm /turn
Acceleration:	1
Deceleration:	1

Battlefield Armoured Personnel Carriers

Used for rapid squad redeployment on the battlefield.

Carrier 209

Hull Type:	KAGA mk IV-4b
Chassis Type:	Wheeled KAGA mk XIV-e
Handling Class:	3
Top Speed Band:	Speed Band 3
Max. Speed:	480mm /turn
Acceleration:	1
Deceleration:	2

Sand Carrier 4

Hull Type:	KAGA mk IV-4b
Chassis Type:	Wheeled KAGA mk XXII-d
Handling Class:	3
Top Speed Band:	Speed Band 3
Max. Speed:	400mm /turn
Acceleration:	1
Deceleration:	2

Cloud Carrier 405

Hull Type:	KAGA mk IV-4b
Chassis Type:	Hover KAGA mk IX-n
Handling Class:	2
Top Speed Band:	Speed Band 3
Max. Speed:	480mm /turn
Acceleration:	1
Deceleration:	1

Battletanks

The general purpose battlefield vehicle.

Nomad V4

Hull Type:	KAGA mk X-2
Chassis Type:	Wheeled KAGA mk XIV-e
Handling Class:	3
Top Speed Band:	Speed Band 2
Max. Speed:	320mm /turn
Acceleration:	1
Deceleration:	2

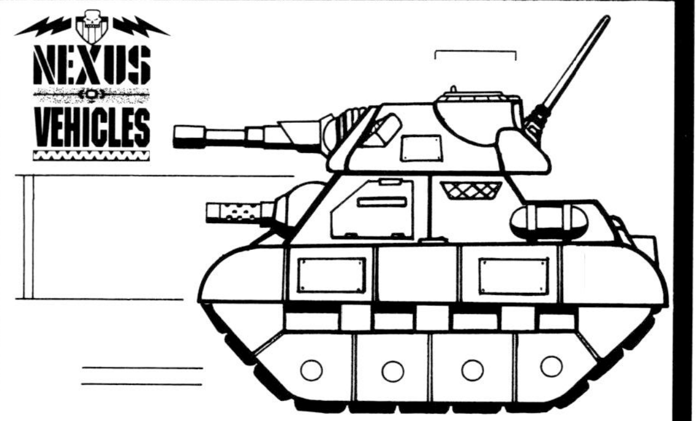

Assegai

Assegai

Hull Type:	KAGA mk X-2
Chassis Type:	Tracked KAGA mk XXII-d
Handling Class:	1
Top Speed Band:	Speed Band 2
Max. Speed:	240mm /turn
Acceleration:	1
Deceleration:	2

Thundercloud

Hull Type:	KAGA mk X-2
Chassis Type:	Hover KAGA mk IX-n
Handling Class:	1
Top Speed Band:	Speed Band 2
Max. Speed:	320mm /turn
Acceleration:	1
Deceleration:	1

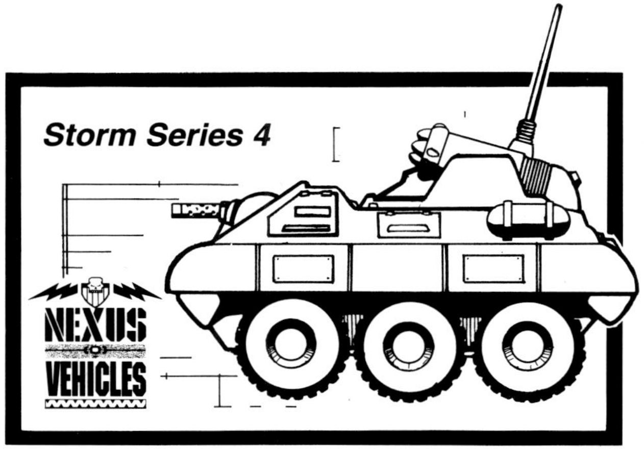

Rocket Launchers

Mobile support with general use firepower.

Storm Series IV

Hull Type:	KAGA mk VIII-11e
Chassis Type:	Wheeled KAGA mk XIV-e
Handling Class:	3
Top Speed Band:	Speed Band 3
Max. Speed:	400mm /turn
Acceleration:	1
Deceleration:	2

Darkstorm Series III

Hull Type:	KAGA mk VIII-11e
Chassis Type:	Tracked KAGA mk XXII-d
Handling Class:	3
Top Speed Band:	Speed Band 2
Max. Speed:	320mm /turn
Acceleration:	1
Deceleration:	2

Cloud-Dart II

Hull Type:	KAGA mk VIII-11e
Chassis Type:	Hover KAGA mk IX-n
Handling Class:	2
Top Speed Band:	Speed Band 3
Max. Speed:	400mm /turn
Acceleration:	1
Deceleration:	1

Striders

Striders have become the masters of the battlefield. They combine rapid movement with heavy armour and weapons to produce a powerful synthesis.

There are only two different families of strider. The first and by far the most prolific is that made by the Hajunka subsidiary MOA - the Storm Strider series.

The other family of machines is that built by the small independent RAVEN Corporation - though its striders also use a MOA bipedal chassis.

Storm Striders

All current Hajunka Storm Striders use the MOA BBC mkII-7 bipedal chassis but have different hulls, armour and armament specifications.

Gladiator

Mass:	16
Size:	13
Crew:	2
Chassis:	MOA BBC mk II-7
Hull:	Swivel Arc of 45° either side of the direction of movement.
Armour:	15mm iridio-steel laminated with beryllium bronze (AC 7 - Hard)
Primary Weapon:	twin fixed mounted HAK 1000 Auto-Machine Cannon.
Secondary Weapon:	single hull mounted HAK B17 fm Light Machine Gun with a45° Fire Arc.
Handling Class:	3
Top Speed Band:	Speed Band 3
Max. Speed:	400mm /turn
Acceleration:	1
Deceleration:	2

Goliath

Mass:	17
Size:	13
Crew:	2
Chassis:	MOA BBC mk II-7
Hull:	Swivel Arc of 45° either side of the direction of movement.
Armour:	20mm iridio-steel laminated with beryllium bronze (AC4 - Hard]
Armament:	twin fixed mounted HAK 1010 Cannons.
Handling Class:	2

Top Speed Band:	Speed Band 3
Max. Speed:	320mm /turn
Acceleration:	1
Deceleration:	2

Fenris

Mass:	15
Size:	13
Crew:	2
Chassis:	MOA BBC mk II-7
Hull:	Swivel Arc of 45° either side of the direction of movement.
Armour:	15mm iridio-steel crystallated with ceramic filaments (AC 10 - Hard)
Primary Weapon:	triple fixed mounted Kotor ACG12 Assault Chain-Cannons.
Handling Class:	3
Top Speed Band:	Speed Band 3
Max. Speed:	480mm /turn
Acceleration:	1
Deceleration:	2

Valkyrie

Mass:	15
Size:	13
Crew:	3
Chassis:	MOA BBC mk II-7
Hull:	Swivel Arc of 45° either side of the direction of movement.
Armour:	15mm iridio-steel crystallated with ceramic filaments.

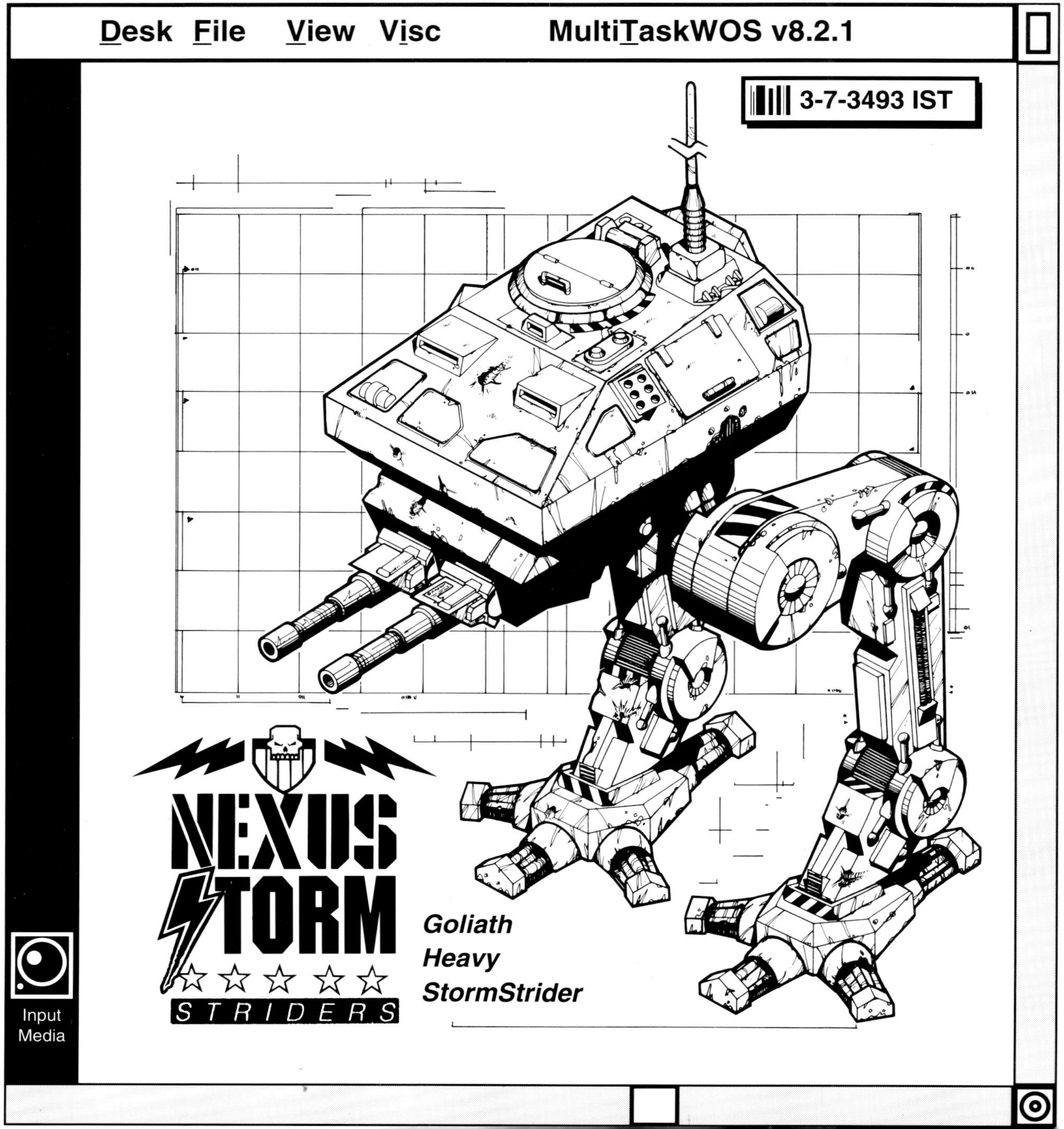

Desk File View T v8

Input Media

Raven Scavenger
Aleph 2.1

Armour (cont):	(AC 10 - Hard)
Primary Weapon:	twin fixed mounted Kotor ACG5 Chain-gun.
Secondary Weapon:	two independently hull mounted HAK B17 fm Light Machine Gun with a 45° Fire Arc.
Handling Class:	3
Top Speed Band:	Speed Band 3
Max. Speed:	480mm /turn
Acceleration:	2
Deceleration:	2

Tiamat

Mass:	16
Size:	13
Crew:	2
Chassis:	MOA BBC mk II-7
Hull:	Swivel Arc of 45° either side of the direction of movement.
Armour:	15mm iridio-steel laminated with beryllium bronze (AC 7 - Hard)
Primary Weapon:	twin fixed mounted BAT 23 Napalm Cannons.
Handling Class:	3
Top Speed Band:	Speed Band 3
Max. Speed:	400mm /turn
Acceleration:	1
Deceleration:	2

The Raven Scavenger Series

The Raven Scavenger series was only released in 3480, nine years after Hajunka's Storm Strider series. They were designed to fill a perceived gap in the spectrum of striders supplied by Hajunka. The Scavenger series expresses an idiosyncratic departure from the more stolid Storm Strider design and is an altogether lighter and faster battlefield system.

In spite of the radical new design the Scavenger series still relies on a MOA biped chassis the BBC mk IX - one specially developed for Raven by MOA and a lighter version of the famous BBC mk II.

Raven (Scavenger Aleph 2.1)

Mass:	12
Size:	10
Crew:	1
Chassis:	MOA BBC mk IX-3
Hull:	Swivel Arc of 45° either side of the direction of movement.
Armour:	10mm iridio-steel surface coated with 2mm of iridio-steel laminated with beryllium bronze (AC 13 - Hard)
Primary Weapon:	three independently mounted Kotor ACG 5 Chain-guns with 45° Fire Arcs.
Secondary Weapon:	twin fixed mounted HAK B17 fm Light Machine Guns.
Handling Class:	4
Top Speed Band:	Speed Band 4
Max. Speed:	560mm /turn
Acceleration:	2
Deceleration:	2

Raven II (Raven Scavenger Beta)

Mass:	12
Size:	10
Crew:	1
Chassis:	MOA BBC mk IX-3
Hull:	Swivel Arc of 45° either side of the direction of movement.
Armour:	10mm iridio-steel surface coated with 2mm of iridio-steel laminated with beryllium bronze (AC 13 - Hard)
Primary Weapon:	twin fixed mounted Vector 12 (V12) missile systems.
Secondary Weapon:	twin fixed mounted HAK B17 fm Light Machine Guns.
Handling Class:	4
Top Speed Band:	Speed Band 4
Max. Speed:	560mm /turn
Acceleration:	2
Deceleration:	2

Cybernetic Battlefield Units

Although cybernetics has been a part of military technology for centuries it was only in the 3470s that a fully operational independent cybernetic battlefield system was possible. The key enabling technology was the Agarax Cyberneural Matrix - the ACM X1 which was developed by Cerebex for the Agarax Megacorp in 3472.

Talos CBU	
Mass:	**1**
Size:	**3**
Control System:	**ACM series X5**
Chassis:	**Talos mk.1**
Hand Held Weapons:	**GG-14: Gauss Rifle / Grenade Launcher, T-109: Twin Hak-109 Combat Rifles and/or T- 420 / 109: combination Hak-420 Recoilless Rifle / 109 Combat Rifle**
Propulsion System:	**2 Tokomak Ring Reactors**
Armour:	**Beryllium bronze plated iridio-steel shell. (AC 4-Soft)**
Move :	**Normal=150 Impetus=D10x10+10 Charge=200**

Talos Unit.
Armed with **Ksirus Intergrated Cybermount** left arm. (This example houses twin mounted **HAK B17(gm)**.) and a **Ksirus integrated sidearm (GG-14)**.

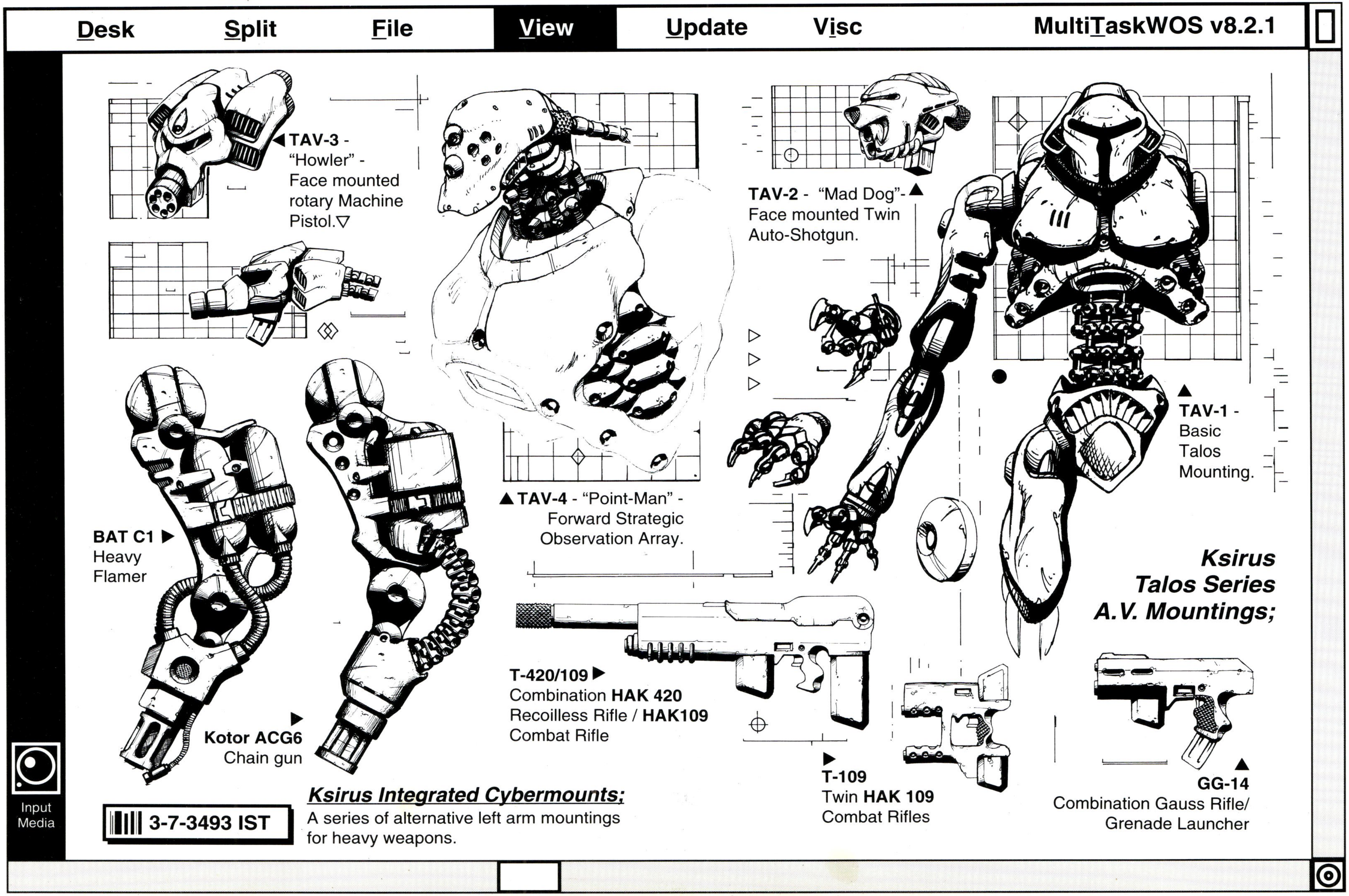
Desk
Split
File
View
Update
Visc
MultiTaskWOS v8.2.1
Ksirus
Talos Series
A.V. Mountings;
TAV-1 -
Basic
Talos
Mounting.
TAV-2 - "Mad Dog"-
Face mounted Twin
Auto-Shotgun.
TAV-3 -
"Howler" -
Face mounted
rotary Machine
Pistol.
TAV-4 - "Point-Man" -
Forward Strategic
Observation Array.
BAT C1
Heavy
Flamer
Kotor ACG6
Chain gun
T-420/109
Combination HAK 420
Recoilless Rifle / HAK109
Combat Rifle
T-109
Twin HAK 109
Combat Rifles
GG-14
Combination Gauss Rifle/
Grenade Launcher
Ksirus Integrated Cybermounts;
A series of alternative left arm mountings
for heavy weapons.
3-7-3493 IST
Input
Media

The Ksirus Helcat

The first CBU to see active service in the Nexus armed forces was the Helcat series produced by the Agarax subsidiary Ksirus. The Hajunka subsidiary MOA were commissioned to develop BBC mk VIII which was a smaller version of the BBC mk II series biped chassis. The Helcat was actually called the Ks BWP series but early on in tests the screaming of its exhausts as it engaged led the researchers to nickname it the "Hellcat". Ksirus bowed to the inevitable and named the series Helcat instead.

The MOA BBC mk VIII-2

The MOA BBC mk VIII-2 series of bipedal battlefield weapons platforms was produced expressly for Ksirus to experiment with its new ACMs. The experiments were highly successful and the 'Helcat' series cybernetic battlefield unit went into service in 3474.

The Ksirus BWP

The Ksirus standard BWP is built around the MOA BBC mk VIII-2 chassis and includes an armoured turret. It is powered by a single high-yield fusion reactor. The turret carries twin fixed mounted HAK A20 sub-machine guns as standard.

Cerberus

Mass:	1
Size:	3
Control System:	**ACM series X2**
Chassis:	**MOA BBC mk 8-2**
Turret:	**swivel arc of 45° to either side of the direction of movement.**
Primary Weapons:	**2 fixed wing-mounted Spindal 100 gauss cannons.**
Secondary Weapons:	**2 fixed mounted HAK A20 sub-machine guns.**
Propulsion System:	**Tokomak Ring Reactor**
Armour:	**Iridio-steel plated Weave-Shell (AC 7-Soft)**

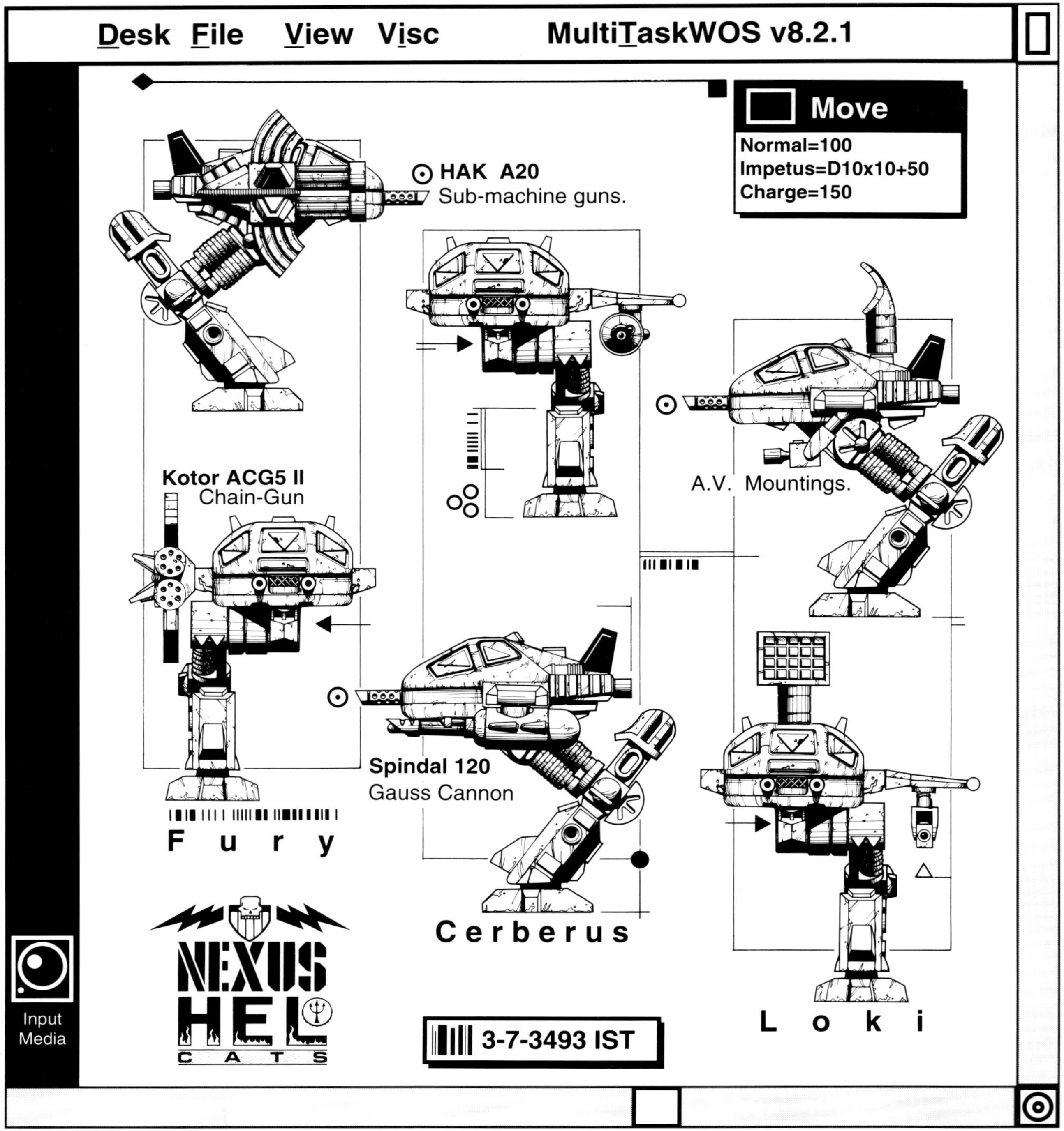

Loki

Mass:	1
Size:	3
Control System:	ACM series X2
Chassis:	MOA BBC mk 8-2
Turret:	swivel arc of 45° to either side of the direction of movement.
Primary Function:	Integrated remote sensing units functional up to Medium Range.
Secondary Weapons:	2 fixed mounted HAK A20 sub-machine guns.
Propulsion System:	Tokomak Ring Reactor
Armour:	Iridio-steel plated Weave-Shell (AC 7-Soft)

Fury

Mass:	1
Size:	3
Control System:	ACM series X2
Chassis:	MOA BBC mk 8-2
Turret:	swivel arc of 45° to either side of the direction of movement.
Primary Weapons:	2 twin wing-mounted Kotor ACG5 Chain-Cannons.
Secondary Weapons:	2 fixed mounted HAK A20 sub-machine guns.
Propulsion System:	Tokomak Ring Reactor
Armour:	Iridio-steel plated Weave-Shell (AC 7-Soft)

Buildings - Descriptions

The Nexus Military have a range of modular battlefront buildings. Some are constructed on site while others are dropped by stratotugs to form the front line of defence.

Command Bunkers

The nerve centres of any battlefront architecture. Two standard forms A and B.

Mass:	35
Size:	26
Crew:	4
Armour:	1000mm Ceramic Blend (AC 5 - Hard)
Primary Function (A):	One Extreme, Long and Medium Range Sensors
Primary Function (B):	Turret Mounted HAK 1010 Cannon. Firing Arc restricted (see model)
Secondary Function (A):	Sentinel Turret with twin fixed mounted HAK B17fm Light Machine Guns. Firing Arc restricted (see model)
Secondary Function (B):	Turret with Vector 12 Missile System. Firing Arc restricted (see model)
Accessways:	3 environmental locks.
Extra Crew Capacity:	5

Heavy Gun Bunkers

Fixed Heavy Gun Emplacements. Four standard forms A, B, C & D. All have unrestricted Firing Arcs.

Mass:	34
Size:	24
Crew:	3
Armour:	1000mm Ceramic Blend (AC 5 - Hard)
Primary Function (A):	Turret mounted HAK 2000 Howitzer.
Primary Function (B):	Turret mounted HAK 4000 Auto-Cannon.
Primary Function (C):	Turret mounted Vector 7 "Flamedart" Missile System.
Primary Function (D):	Twin turret mounted Vector 12 (V12) Missile System.
Accessways:	1 environmental locks.
Extra Crew Capacity:	none

Light Gun Bunkers

Fixed Light Gun Emplacements. Two standard forms A & B. Both have restricted Firing Arcs (see model).

Mass:	20
Size:	15
Crew:	2
Armour:	500mm Ceramic Blend (AC 10 - Hard)

Primary Function (A):	Two Security Turrets each with twin HAK B17 fm Machine Guns.
Primary Function (B):	Two Sentinel Turrets one with twin and the other with single HAK B17 fm Machine Guns.
Accessways:	1 environmental locks.
Extra Crew Capacity:	none

Towers

Elevated Platforms for Heavy Gun Sensor installations. Four standard forms A, B, C & D. All have unrestricted Firing Arcs.

Mass:	27
Size:	20
Crew:	1
Armour:	500mm Ceramic Blend (AC 10 - Hard)
Primary Function (A):	One each of Extreme, Long and Medium Range Sensors.
Primary Function (B):	Turret mounted HAK 4000 Auto-Cannon
Primary Function (C):	Turret mounted Vector 7 "Flamedart" Missile System.
Primary Function (D):	Twin turret mounted Vector 12 (V12) Missile System.
Accessways:	3 environmental locks.
Extra Crew Capacity:	5

Advance GunTowers

These towers are dropped to forward positions from Stratospheric Craft. They have a standard stabilizing hydraulic quadropod. Three standard forms A, B & C. All have unrestricted Firing Arcs.

Mass:	19
Size:	14
Crew:	1
Armour:	370mm Ceramic Alloy with Beryllium Bronze (AC 10 - Hard)
Primary Function (A):	Turret mounted HAK 1010 Cannon
Primary Function (B):	Turret mounted HAK 1000 Auto-Machine Cannon
Primary Function (C):	Twin turret mounted Vector 12 (V12) Missile System.
Accessways:	Hatch
Extra Crew Capacity:	none

Micro Gun Towers

Smaller versions of Advance Gun Towers, however these are fully automated. Two standard forms A & B. All have unrestricted Firing Arcs.

Mass:	11
Size:	8
Crew:	0
Armour:	45mm Ceramic Alloy with Beryllium Bronze (AC 16 - Hard)

Primary Function (A):	One Security Turrets with twin HAK B17 fm Machine Guns.
Primary Function (B):	One Sentinel Turrets one with twin or single HAK B17 fm Machine Guns.
Accessways:	none
Extra Crew Capacity:	none

Squad Bunker

Squad refuge in hostile environments. Standard form.

Mass:	27
Size:	20
Crew:	none
Armour:	700mm Ceramic Blend (AC 7 - Hard)
Primary Function:	Sentinel Turret with single mounted HAK B17fm Light Machine Gun with unrestricted Fire Arc.
Accessways:	2 environmental locks
Extra Crew Capacity:	10

Landing Pad

Landing Pad for one man vertical take off stratospheric vehicle. Standard form.

Mass:	27
Size:	20
Crew:	1
Armour:	500mm Ceramic Blend (AC 10 - Hard)
Primary Function:	Landing Pad
Accessways:	1 environmental lock
Extra Crew Capacity:	none

Hospital Dome

Battlefield Emergency Treatment Centre for up to three casualties. Standard form.

Mass:	34
Size:	24
Crew:	3 (medical personnel)
Armour:	500mm Ceramic Blend (AC 10 - Hard)
Primary Function:	Receiving wounded.
Accessways:	3 environmental locks
Extra Crew Capacity:	10

Power Dome

Power Generator for sustaining larger modular complexes. Standard form.

Mass:	21
Size:	16
Crew:	1
Armour:	1000mm Ceramic Blend (AC 5 - Hard)
Primary Function:	Tokomak Double Ring Fusion Reactor
Accessways:	1 environmental lock
Extra Crew Capacity:	none

Missile Silos

Used for launching strategic and anti-missile missiles. Two forms A & B.

Mass (A):	25
Mass (B):	12
Size (A):	19
Size (B):	9
Crew:	automated
Armour:	1000mm Ceramic Blend (AC 5 - Hard)
Primary Function (A):	Strategic missiles
Primary Function (B):	anti-missile missiles
Accessways:	hatch
Extra Crew Capacity:	none

Linking Corridors

Two forms A & B.

Mass:	12
Size:	9
Crew:	none
Armour:	500mm Ceramic Blend (AC 10 - Hard)
Primary Function (A):	Two way access link
Primary Function (B):	3-way access link
Extra Crew Capacity:	5

Desk Split File View Update Visc MultiTaskWOS v8.2.1

Kryomek Helion

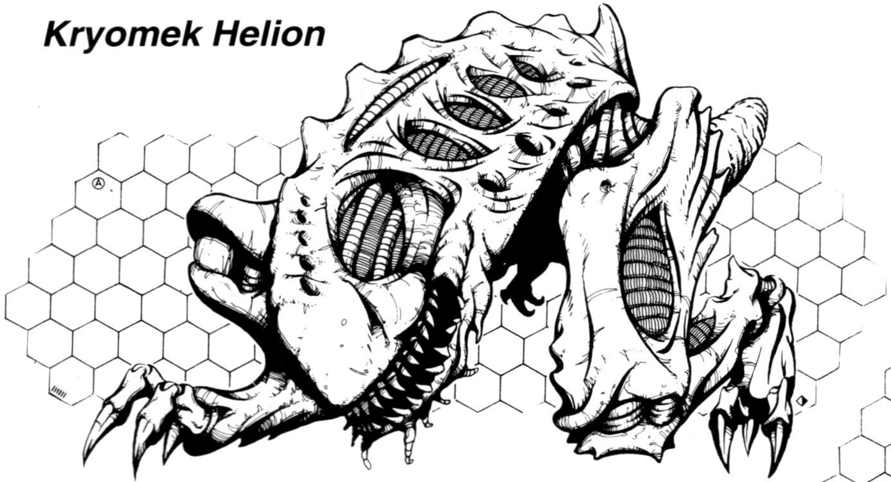

HELION

Size :	3
AC :	8
RC :	N/A
CC :	9

CC ATTACKS	STRIKE	IMP
1 x ARM	0	+3

Kryomek Warrior armed with **Bioacid Spray** and **Single-Molecule Blade**.

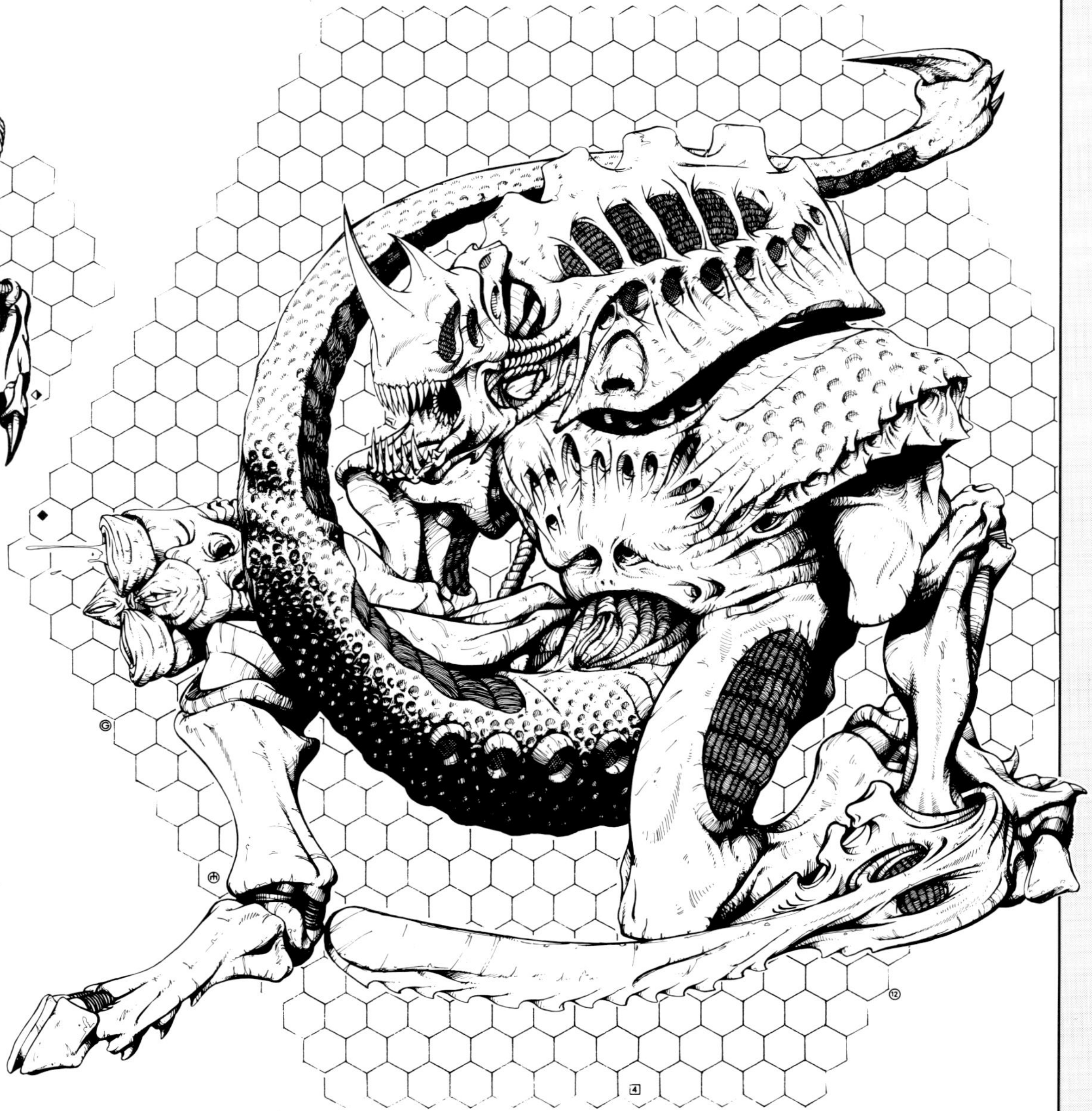

WARRIOR

Size :	5
AC :	4
RC :	8
CC :	12

CC ATTACKS	STRIKE	IMP
2 x ARM	0	+1

Input Media

3-7-3493 IST

Desk Split File View Update Visc MultiTaskWOS v8.2.1

Kryomek Warmaster
armed with Single-Molecule Cleaver and Plasmid Cloud Duster.

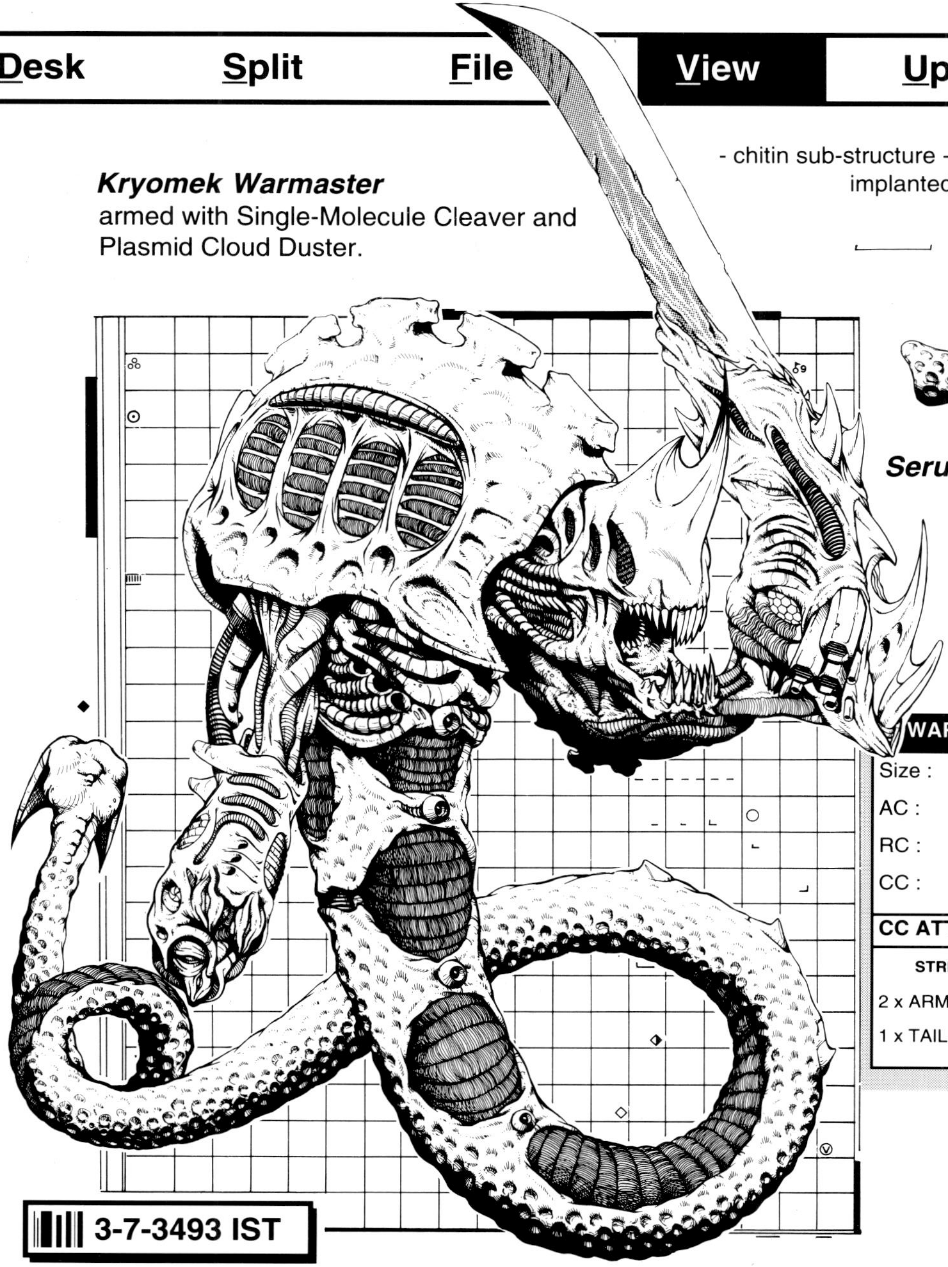

WARMASTER	
Size :	6
AC :	2
RC :	9
CC :	15

CC ATTACKS	STRIKE	IMP
2 x ARM	0	+2
1 x TAIL	-2	+3

Single-Molecule Blade

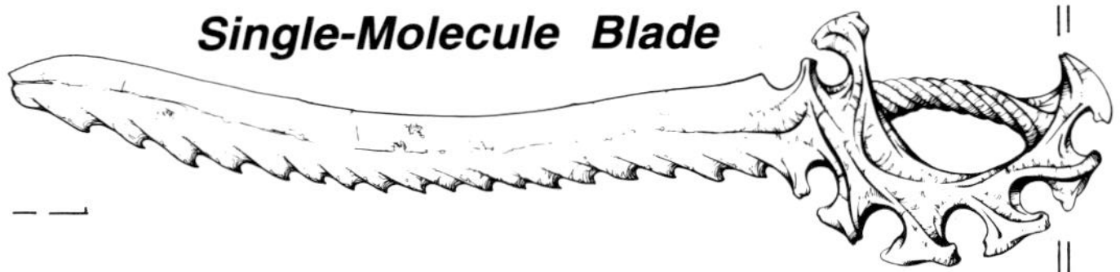

- chitin sub-structure - multiple serration implanted molecule-chains.

Serumic Bioacid Jet

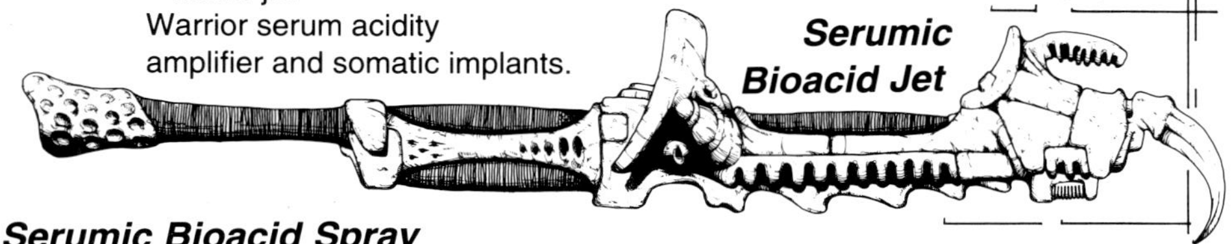

- mono-jet -
Warrior serum acidity amplifier and somatic implants.

Serumic Bioacid Spray

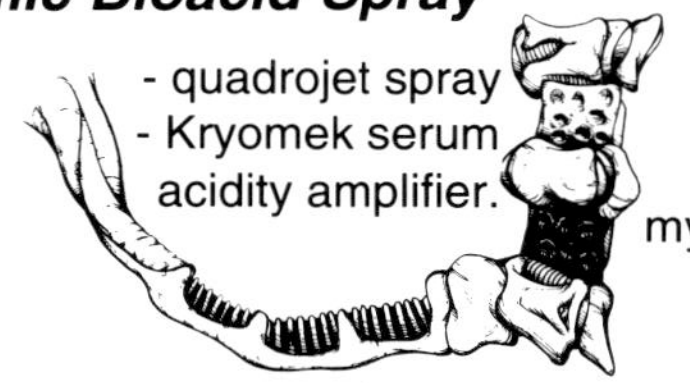

- quadrojet spray
- Kryomek serum acidity amplifier.

Spore Launcher

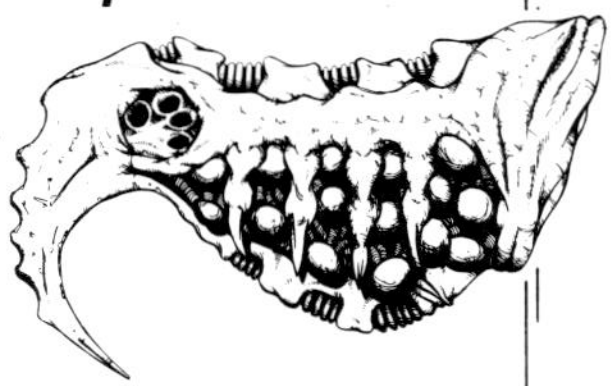

- hyper-metabolic necrotopic mycelia spore projector from regenerative organocartridges.

Plasmid Cloud Duster

- aerosolic jet - projects particles infected from Warmaster

Single-Molecule Cleaver

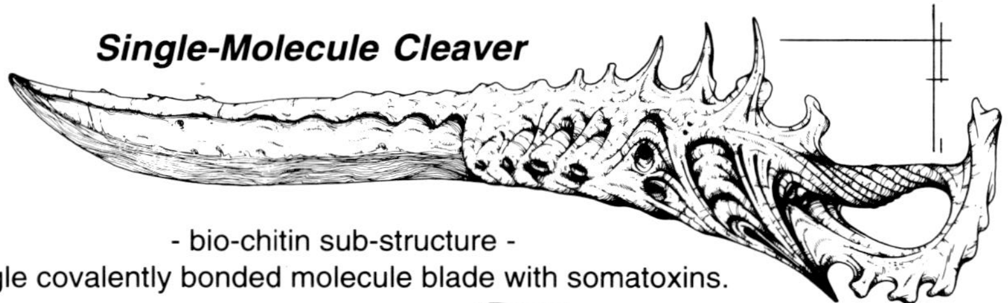

- bio-chitin sub-structure -
single covalently bonded molecule blade with somatoxins.

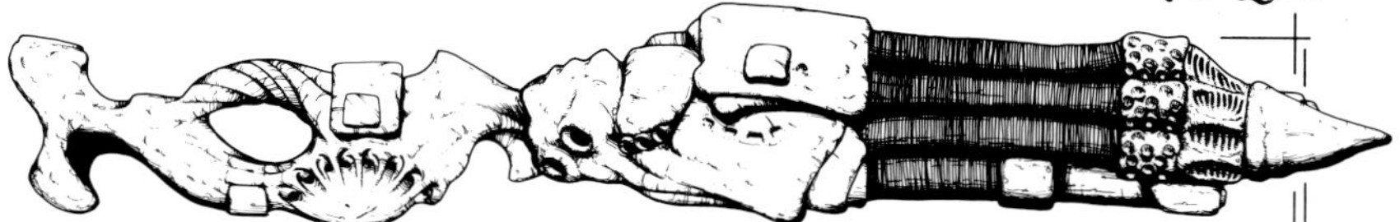

Corroder Lance
- multi-jet mixing - Warmaster serum acidity and somatic implants - variable corrosive gradient.

Nexus Weapons

Personnel Weapons	Close Combat		Short		Medium		Long		Extreme		RANGE BAND		
	Strike	Rank	Targetting	Rank	Targetting	Rank	Targetting	Rank	Targetting	Rank	Target Armour	Impact	Notes
Auto-Pistol	0	1	-	-	-	-	-	-	-	-	S	-1	
Machine-Pistol	+4	2	+2	2	-	-	-	-	-	-	S	0	
Sub-Machine Gun	+3	2	+2	2	-	-	-	-	-	-	S	0	2H
Combat Rifle	0	1	+2	1	0	1	-3	1	-	-	S	+1	2H
Gauss Rifle	0	1	+3	1	+1	1	-2	1	-	-	S	+2	2H
Auto-Shotgun	+2	1	+2	2	-	-	-	-	-	-	S	+1	2H
Xenoid Stick	-2	1	-	-	-	-	-	-	-	-	S	+4	
Light Machine Gun (Gyro)	0	1	+2	3	-3	2	-	-	-	-	S	+3	2H
Chain Gun (Gyro)	+1	1	+4	3	-1	2	-	-	-	-	S	+4	2H
Recoilless Rifle (S.A.P.)	0	1	0	1	-2	1	-4	1	-	-	S	+6	2H
(H.A.P.)	0	1	0	1	-2	1	-4	1	-	-	H	-2	2H
Grenade Launcher	-	-	0	-	-3	-	-	-	-	-	S	+2	T,IF
Heavy Flamer	-	-	0	-	-	-	-	-	-	-	S	+4	2H,T
Light Flamer	-	-	0	-	-	-	-	-	-	-	S	+4	2H,T

T = Template Effect. **IF** = Indirect Fire Capability. 2H= Two-Handed

Fixed Mounted Weapons	Close Combat		Short		Medium		Long		Extreme				
	Strike	Rank	Targetting	Rank	Targetting	Rank	Targetting	Rank	Targetting	Rank	Target Armour	Impact	Notes
Gauss Cannon	0	1	+3	1	+1	1	-2	1	-	-	S	+3	
Light Machine Gun	+1	1	+1	3	-1	3	-3	2	-5	1	S	+3	
Chain Gun	0	1	+2	3	0	3	-2	2	-4	1	S	+4	
Strip Missile	-	-	-	-	-	-	-2	-	-3	-	S	+6	S8,U
	-	-	-	-	-	-	-2	-	-3	-	H	-2	S8,U
Napalm Cannon	-	-	+1	-	-1	-	-3	-	-5	-	S	+5	T
Chain Cannon	-	-	+1	-	-1	-	-3	-	-6	-	S	+4	T
	-	-	+1	-	-1	-	-3	-	-6	-	H	-6	T
Machine Cannon (SAP)	-	-	+1	-	-1	-	-3	-	-5	-	S	+6	T,X
(HAP)	-	-	+1	-	-1	-	-3	-	-5	-	H	0	X
Cannon (SAP)	-	-	0	-	-1	-	-3	-	-4	-	S	+8	T,X
(HAP)	-	-	0	-	-1	-	-3	-	-4	-	H	+4	X
Cluster Missiles	-	-	-1	-	-1	-	-2	-	-4	-	S	+3	T
	-	-	-1	-	-1	-	-2	-	-4	-	H	-4	T
Howitzer	-	-	-	-	-	-	-4	-	-3	-	S	+6	T,IF,U
	-	-	-	-	-	-	-4	-	-3	-	H	-2	T,IF
Auto-Cannon(SAP)	-	-	-	-	-3	-	0	-	-3	-	S	+8	T,U
(HAP)	-	-	-	-	-3	-	0	-	-3	-	H	+2	T
Storm Strider Stomp Attack	0	1	-	-	-	-	-	-	-	-	S	+8	

X = Either H.A.P. ***or*** S.A.P. Round. **T** =Template Effect. **IF** =Indirect Fire Capability.
S8 =Minimum Size of Target (Size 8). **U** =Unlimited Range, treat as Extreme range for Targetting

Kryomek Weapons

Kryomek Weapons	Close Combat		Short		Medium		Long		Extreme		RANGE BAND		
	Strike	Rank	Targetting	Rank	Targetting	Rank	Targetting	Rank	Targetting	Rank	Target Armour	Impact	Notes
Plasmid Cloud Duster	+3	2	0	-	-	-	-	-	-	-	S	+2	T
Bio-Acid Jet	-	-	0	-	-	-	-	-	-	-	S	+6	2H,T
	-	-	0	-	-	-	-	-	-	-	H	+2	T
Bio-Acid Spray (Close)	+2	2	-	-	-	-	-	-	-	-	S	+1	
Bio-Acid Spray (Ranged)	-	-	0	-	-	-	-	-	-	-	S	+4	T
Corroder Lance (Close)	0	3	-	-	-	-	-	-	-	-	S	+6	2H
	0	1	-	-	-	-	-	-	-	-	H	+4	
Corroder Lance (Ranged)	-	-	0	-	-	-	-	-	-	-	S	+8	2H,T
	-	-	0	-	-	-	-	-	-	-	H	+4	T
Spore Launcher	-	-	0	-	-2	-	-4	-	-6	-	S	+3	2H,T,IF
	-	-	0	-	-2	-	-4	-	-6	-	H	-2	T,IF
Single-Molecule Blade	+1	2	-	-	-	-	-	-	-	-	S	+3	
	+1	1	-	-	-	-	-	-	-	-	H	-4	
Single Molecule Cleaver	+1	2	-	-	-	-	-	-	-	-	S	+4	
	+1	1	-		-	-	-	-	-	-	H	-2	

T = Template Effect. **IF** = Indirect Fire Capability. **2H**= Two-Handed

CHAPTER 11

APPENDICES

Appendix A: Dimensional Manifolds

A Dimensional Manifold or Diman is a structure of space that links together several points that are distant in spacetime. These points, the entrances to the diman, are called interstices and though these move in spacetime they can be located using probability mathematics.

Spacefolding equipment can be used to open the interstice and allow a spaceship to pass through the diman. More probability mathematics is used to choose one of the possible exits from the diman. Diman transportation is virtually instantaneous.

Appendix B: Dimensional Manifolds (Technical)

A **Trans-Dimensional Manifold** or simply a **Dimensional Manifold** or in common usage, a **Diman** is a structure of 13 dimensional space that transcends the four dimensions of space and time.

A diman is categorised by having a number of **pseudo-points** which within the diman are effectively a single point. Each pseudo-point has a manifestation in spacetime which is termed an **interstice**. At these interstices the diman is **continuous** with spacetime. The interstices drift in spacetime though their position can be determined by using probability mathematics.

An interstice is an opening into the diman which would be traversable by a black hole singularity. To allow larger entities to enter it a section of spacetime must be **folded** and passed through the singularity. This has been achieved by producing a black micro-hole around the interstice and allowing it to instantaneously collapse. The effect of this is to fold a hypersphere of spacetime with hyperdiameter proportional to the macrodiameter of the black micro-hole. This is whiplashed through the singularity into the diman.

Though effectively all pseudo-points in the diman are identified to a single hyperspatial point, they do actually shear to form every possible pairing of two pseudo-points. Which of these shear trajectories are accessed is determined by a probability-pattern of gravitational eddies generated by the spacefolding process. In effect this means that if these patterns are set up in a particular way the entity will pass into and out of the diman in a controlled way and thus make a jump between two of its interstices.

These shear trajectories are classified according to the mean distance between their two corresponding interstices in space-time.

Type	*Mean Distance*
0	**1 parsec**
1	**2 parsecs**
2	**4 parsecs**
3	**16 parsecs**
4	**256 parsecs**
5	**65536 parsecs**
6	**4294967296 parsecs**

Appendix C: Megacorps

Pandaris Prime

Pandaris Prime finances huge research projects in the field of psycho-communications. It pioneered and now monopolises the probability mapping of dimensional manifolds. The Megacorp has made notable advances in historio-mathematics and psycho-historical control theory.

Agarax

The primary user and developer of cybernetic technologies, Agarax believes that Man's destiny lies in robotics.

Cerabex

An Agarax subsidiary which developed and now manufactures the Agarax Cyberneural Matrix.

Ksirus

A subsidiary of Agarax which manufactures bipedal battlefield vehicles. Its profitability soared with the release of the Talos Series Battlefield Unit.

Vector Space Developments

This is a missile development company best known for its battlefield missile weapons: the V7 "flamedart" and the V12.

Hajunka

Hajunka, perhaps the biggest of all Megacorps, specialises in heavy industrial structures. It has a panhumanic monopoly in the construction of the big diman (dimensional manifold) spaceships. In spite of this, its most famous product is the space folding equipment that has allowed Man to colonise the Galaxy.

MOA

This Hajunka subsidiary manufactures specialised transport systems. Probably their best known products are the wide range of bipedal battle chassis which are becoming such an important part of the Nexus military machine.

Hardon & Kluvis

The weapons division of Hajunka is the main producer of the standard issue light, medium and heavy equipment for the Nexus. Its name is synonymous with the HAK 109 Series rifle.

Bitarkis

This Megacorp specialises in bio-genetic technologies. Initially it started as an agro-genetic combine. Later it began moving into sophisticated bio-somatic remodelling of livestock strains. Most recently the Megacorp has begun to experiment with humano-somatic remodelling.

Biagrotech

Initially a company producing complex and exotic agricultural equipment it has now become effectively the Bitarkis weapons division. It produces chemical and bio-chemical weaponry such as the BAT mina (muscilated isoton - napalm) series 23 cannon

Appendix D: "Cyclos"

Sentence-enrollment into the Convict Special Forces is mandatory for criminals of green PCB rating or higher - though it is only quite recently that this has been extended from the yellow into the green categories of offenders. Once a citizen becomes a cyclo it is unlikely that he or she will ever return into civilian life.

On enrollment the criminal becomes a cyclo by the dual processes of neural-regulation and addictive systemic poisoning. Both of these are theoretically reversible.

The neural-regulator device is implanted in the forehead and forms transient neuro-linkages with the subject's cortex. It also acts as a receiver for control signals from the unit's centurion. It allows the cyclo's basic metabolic and several of his higher functions to be controlled. Cyclo units can easily be put into battle frenzy and the access that the neuro-regulator provides to both the pain and pleasure centres makes them obedient to the wills of their centurions.

The systemic poison administered to the subject on enrollment is byzantanol tetraprolene which unless it is neutralised with regular doses of Tantha (erzolar caxumate) - its natural antidote -will cause the subject to experience accelerating nervous system disfunction which will eventually lead to complete systemic collapse and death. This ensures that each individual cyclo has a vested interest in keeping the chain of command intact so that it can continue to regularly deliver the antidote.

Demobilisation is possible for cyclos that have performed some exceptional service beyond that required of them. This has never happened for a red category cyclo.

Appendix E: Terms in common usage

admiral	task force commander
ACG	Assault Chain Gun
ACM	Active Cyberneural Matrix
b-squad	military unit of 10 men
bicention	military unit of 200 men
bicenturion	commander of a bicention
bimyriad	military unit of 2000 men
bimyricom	commander of a bimyriad
BWP	Battlefield Weapons Platforms
cention	military unit of 100 men
centurion	commander of a cention
DBCR	Department of Battlefield Cryogenic Research.
diman	Dimensional Manifold
dreadnought	task force unit with both trans-dimensional jumping and diman capabilities.
hegemony	a political grouping of independent states with one state acting as the leader.
I-Class	Refers to planets that are of the Irallic type and perfect for humanic habitation.
IST	Irallic Standard Time
ISY	Irallic Standard Year
Metaconomy	the panhumanic economic complex
myriad	military unit of 1000 men
myricom	commander of a myriad
NCSS	Nexus Centre for Strategic Studies
NMI	Nexus Military Intelligence
panhumanic	'of the whole of humanity'
PCB	Penal Classification Band
quorumate	Ruling committee with a fixed number of members.
squad	military unit of 5 men
stratecom	military commander
strategion	a military force consisting of more than two myriad
Talosic	of the Talos Series Battlefield Unit - generally this term refers to stand alone cybernetic systems with a high level of integrated responses and reactions.
TCDS	Tri-planetary Centre for Demographic Studies.
TDC	Trans-Dimensional Carrier

klik
klik
klik
klik
klik
klik
KLIK!
KLIK!
KLIK!